For Margaret and Lucy

Strategic Leadership: Essential Concepts

Edward A. Merritt, PhD

Contents

Chapter 01:

Leadership

Introduction

The purpose of the first chapter is to introduce current theories concerning the subject of Leadership and provide a working definition for the topic. I present several models to help provide a useful framework for conceptualizing leadership. You will notice that leadership revolves around involvement with people, as leadership is a social process. How we relate to others in groups is central to understanding key elements of leadership. I review familiar concepts of leadership style as well as theories that relate to followers' ability to follow and the leaders' ability to adopt behavioral styles that maximize the potential for effective leader-follower relations.

Situational Leadership uses four classifications, which range across a spectrum from a high degree of direction to a high degree of delegation. Situational leadership suggests that leaders have a preferred (default) style and there is one style is most appropriate to a given situation. This given situation varies widely based on the capabilities of the followers.

The Grid Model provides a way of looking at behavior and leadership effectiveness with certain leadership styles. The Situation Model relates follower readiness for a task to the leader's ability to modify his or her style to the follower's readiness. I introduce the concept of power to show how power enhances the effectiveness of leaders. Theory X & Y reveals how an individual's view of others can affect leadership style. Again, all of these theories attempt to frame how people relate to each other. Indeed, leadership is a social process.

I cover the idea of effectiveness in this chapter to introduce how we evaluate leaders. This is often a difficult task. However, one must have a measure of how leaders are performing in order to judge their worth to the organization.

The goal of this chapter is to present various ways of thinking about leadership. You will study several theories and concepts that relate to leadership to help you become familiar with this important element of management.

Background

The study of leadership is difficult. The primary reasons are that it covers many disciplines, and it is vague to the point of being open to a variety of interpretations concerning its meaning. There have been a host of definitions offered for the concept of leadership. The most used definitions in vogue revolve around statements including terms like: influence, induce, group, goals, behavior, effectiveness, environment, leader personality traits, leadership style, follower maturity, situation, and others. These terms help to construct frameworks in identifying primary interacting leadership elements. The aim of developing these frameworks is to identify the essence of leadership. After developing a framework, we form a definition of leadership. Although many definitions exist in the literature, the definition used to describe leadership in this text is most similar to the one proposed by James Burns:

"Leadership is the action of inducing, influencing followers to accomplish certain goals that represent the values, wants and needs, the aspirations and expectations of both leader and follower."

After developing a working definition of leadership, it is logical to try to develop concepts that apply to it. Many theories have attempted to capture the nature of leadership but all seem to have fallen short. Most leadership concepts seek to provide a comprehensive explanation of how and why some leaders perform more effectively than others do. Theory development in this area has not been entirely successful. However, the next few pages will be devoted to presenting an overview of leadership theories and how they may be practically applied.

Framework

The manner in which one obtains a leadership position begins to build a leadership framework. Such frameworks include follower expectations, skills required of the leader, group maturity, and other circumstances. Because of the complexity these variables, some authors tend to oversimplify leadership. For example, researchers often classify leadership into either an autocratic or a democratic framework, or describe the leader as the one in control. These terms have categorized the leader and placed a framework around the concept so that specific labels apply to both leaders and followers. By framing leadership, a particular view develops so that leader and follower relations become clear. Concepts and terms become a descriptive device to help develop an understanding of leadership as a concept.

For example, one term often used to describe a leader is control. It is a common notion that the leader is the one in control of followers and the environment. To investigate this concept it is important to provide an idea of the meaning of the term control within a leadership context. One way to look at this is to understand how a leader gains control. Does the method of gaining control affect the leadership environment? What is control? How does control help influence a group? These questions will need addressing in understanding how control affects the leadership environment. For example, the leader may gain control as the result of tradition. If this is the case, followers will have little to say about who has group control. The follower may accept the tradition without questioning its authority.

Followers may blindly accept all consequences of leader actions without questioning the circumstances. Under these circumstances, followers are subjects under the leader's control. Control may coerce followers and force the will of the leader.

At the other end of the spectrum, we have followers electing their leader. While this leader will also have control, it will be of a much different nature. In this case, the leader becomes authorized, within certain parameters, to control the group. If followers are not willingly controlled, they may have a voice in changing the control factor, if desired. If followers decide not to be controlled by a particular leader, they may change leaders. It should be obvious that the element of control within these two environments is different.

From this example, the context and framework from which one is working are extremely important in developing a concept of leadership. The reason for showing how one variable, such as control, may be viewed is to reveal how a wide variety of elements affect leadership. The general environment becomes a mixed bag of factors that affects how group members and leaders interact. Understanding how leaders and followers interact is very important in understanding leadership.

It is important to identify various facets of leadership to gain an understanding of the leadership environment. It is apparent that creating an exhaustive review of all leadership elements and cause/effect relationships cannot be identified--there are just too many. However, the primary goal of this chapter remains one of identifying essential leadership elements and investigating how they interact. The underlying factor in conducting preliminary work is to isolate those primary elements. The question then becomes: Do leadership elements exist which interact in certain ways to produce leader effectiveness? If these elements exist, can they be identified from situation to situation? If there is some consistency to how these elements interact to produce effective leadership, then we may be able to develop predictive models for effective leadership behavior.

The example of control is only one element, which affects the concept of leadership. Frameworks should identify several key leadership elements to provide a solid base for theory development. If cause/affect relationships can be identified, this is a basis for predicting leader success and effectiveness. The next few pages include some theories and concepts that have been used to explain leadership and to isolate cause/effect relationships in the leadership environment.

Personalized Theories

Armchair Theories. Armchair theories are those that are based on personal experience, conjecture, and personal feelings. This is not to imply that these theories do-not have some valid use and benefits, they may, but the purpose in explaining their origins is to identify the foundations of their claims. One such theory is the Great Man Theory, which might be referred to more appropriately as the Great Person Theory. The Great Man is viewed as one who is above the group; is superhuman, and can handle any situation for which the group may need him. This is a throwback to medieval thinking--men were expected to take charge and rescue damsels in distress. The Great Man possesses the attributes of a hero and heroic traits are the basis of group support. There have been many examples of the Great Man Theory in history: Hercules, King Arthur, etc.

Another armchair theory is the Follower Theory. This theory proposes that the way to become a leader is to be an effective follower. The smart follower becomes a leader because he/she has learned through on-the-job training all the necessary skills to lead the group effectively. This concept places primary importance on the experience of the leader and the leader's ability to relate to group members. This leader's skills have been learned through years of experience and experience is the only manner in which he/she can become qualified and accepted by the group. Examples of this model exist in factories, in corporations that rely on corporate experience, and in work environments where skills must be handed from group member to group member.

The Genius Theory, another armchair theory, promotes a person to a position of leadership and separates the person from the rest of the group members because of his/her innate talents and/or knowledge. This person is a leader by virtue of his/her special talents. Einstein and Babe Ruth are two examples of special talents that exemplify this concept.

These concepts or theories present a line of reasoning that describes how leaders obtain their position of leadership and why they are viewed with esteem, but offers little to identify systematic interactions of leadership elements. There are other concepts that could be classified in the category as Armchair, all having the quality of personal perception based on experience. The value of these concepts is that they do help explain elements of the leadership environment. The fallacy of these concepts is that they fail to develop a sound basis for theory development and consequently a body of reliable information to study the subject. Recently, however, there have been major improvements in developing a body of leadership information.

Leadership Theories and Models

The Grid Model. The grid approach helps in determining a leader's tendencies toward a high concern for both people and production. The Grid Model was originally conceptualized by a University of Ohio research team in the 1950s using terms to describe task-oriented and person-oriented behavior. At about the same time, a group of researchers from Japan established a similar model describing an effective leader as one who is high in both performance behavior and maintenance behavior. They referred to their model as the PM Leadership Theory (Peterson and Misumi). However, it is generally believed that Blake and Moulton propelled it into gaining popularity under terms that described a High High leader. This behavioral system applies to leaders and not to groups. It attempts to identify a leader's behavioral patterns on an X and Y coordinate plane, using two basic variables. These variables were identified as systems-oriented behavior on the Y-axis, and person-oriented behavior on the X-axis. Simply stated, the person-oriented behavior is action directed toward satisfying the needs and preferences of individuals, and systems-oriented behavior is behavior directed toward structuring the work environment to accomplish group goals. The coordinate plane and the variables are shown in Figure 1. Paula Silver described her understanding of the systems/person-oriented scheme as having six categories of specified behavior. Again, the purpose for these classifications is to identify leader behavior (applies to leaders and not to groups).

Systems (also referred to by others as production and or task variables):
1. Production Emphasis--increased production of the group.
2. Initiating Structure--establishment and clarification of rules and policies to govern group actions.
3. Role Assumption--active exercise of the leader's position.

4. Representation--acting as the group's spokesperson, furthering the group's interaction with higher authority.
5. Persuasiveness--refers to having firm convictions, convincing others of one's point of view.
6. Superior Orientation--actions that serve to maintain the group, actions that maintain or increase the leader's position within the group.

These six categories provide a comprehensive view of Y-axis variables. A composite score of systems axis variables is obtained to provide a score for the Y-axis. This score represents a leader's systems oriented behavior.

Relations (also referred to by others as person axis variables):

1. Tolerance of Uncertainty--refers to actions that show the leader has the ability to accept postponement and indefiniteness without becoming upset or anxious.
2. Tolerance of Freedom--allows followers scope for their own decisions, actions, etc.
3. Consideration--expressing friendliness and interest, consulting with group members and attending to their suggestions.
4. Demand Reconciliation--dealing with conflicting demands without becoming upset.
5. Integration--action that serves to maintain a closely-knit group and to resolve conflicts among group participants.
6. Predictive Accuracy--set of behaviors that exhibit the leader's foresight and ability to anticipate outcomes.

A composite score for the relationship axis variables yields the value of the leader's tendency to exhibit person-oriented behavior along the X axis. When the X and Y variables are plotted against one another, patterns may be identified to classify a leader's behavioral style.

Figure 1. The Grid Model

| | Systems Oriented. The Y-axis moves vertically from bottom (low) to top (high) from 0-9 | | | | Person Oriented. The X-axis moves horizontally from left (low) to right (high) from 0-9 | | | | |

	0X-	1X-	2X-	3X-	4X-	5X-	6X-	7X-	8X-	9X-
9Y-										
8Y-										
7Y-										
6Y-										
5Y-										
4Y-										
3Y-										
2Y-										
1Y-										
0Y-										

Managerial Grid (Blake and Moulton). Robert Blake and Jane Moulton applied the managerial grid to develop another behavioral approach to leadership, the Managerial Grid, Figure 2. Their Managerial Grid matrix utilizes the intersection of the grid model, coordinate (O,O), forming a matrix with an axis maximum, and uses what Blake and Moulton refer to as relationship and task variables instead of the systems and person variables. The matrix is formed with specific areas identifying certain behavioral tendencies. Coordinates are used on specific areas of the grid to identify the type of leader who would display high/low, low/high, etc., task/relationship behavior. For example, the (1,1) leader is said to exert minimum effort to sustain the group; they are low-task and low-relationship. The leader with a (9,1) is high-task and low-relationship oriented. This person would be classified as emphasizing efficiency, order, and results, with minimum concern of human relations. The (5,5) category reveals a leader that has an orientation toward adequate performance through the balance of work requirements in maintaining satisfactory morale. The (9,9) leader exhibits high-relationship and high-task behavior and is usually a person that allows people a great deal of freedom and independence in their work. The (1,9) leader pays particular attention to the people in the group but is not oriented toward getting things done. These labels are helpful because they allow one to think in specific terms about a leader's behavioral patterns.

There have been various labels used to describe the two dimensional variables: task and relationship. This text will use the terms, task-oriented (TO) and relationship-oriented (RO), when referring to this theory.

Figure 2. Managerial Grid (Blake and Moulton)

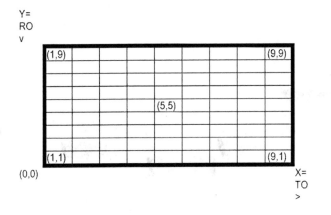

Situational Leadership Contingency Theory (Hersey and Blanchard). The contingency approach to leadership was developed by Paul Hersey and Kenneth Blanchard and applies to both individuals and groups. Essentially, their theory specifies an appropriate leadership style based on the capabilities of the subordinate and or group. A high capability subordinate has the ability and willingness to complete a task successfully. A low capability subordinate lacks both ability and self-confidence to attempt a task.

The model variables are labeled relationship and task and are shown in Figure 3. The contingency model considers both the follower and the leader. It posits that the leader must assess the follower's task readiness before choosing the appropriate relationship behavior. The accurate assessment of the right mix of these two behaviors will yield the most effective leadership style. This assumes that the leader can change his/her behavior (style) and that a change in leadership style will have a maturing effect on the follower. Maturity, at its extremes, means that the follower moves from almost total reliance on the leader for direction and support to the follower developing self-reliance and freedom in performing a task. This model also assumes that the follower's behavior can be changed and that the follower desires his or her behavior to be changed. The essence of the model is that the leader recognizes follower maturity (readiness), and correspondingly chooses an effective leader style.

Hersey and Blanchard characterized leadership style in terms of the amount of direction and support that a leader gives to his or her followers under the classifications: Directing (the highest amount of supervision and control), Coaching, Supporting, and Delegating (the lowest amount of supervision and control).

- Directing. In directing, the leaders define the tasks to be accomplished and supervise them closely. Decisions are made by the leader and communication with followers is mostly one-way from leader to follower or group. Directing is also referred to as autocratic and militaristic.

  The true nature of this concept is not as simple as it seems. What most people usually mean when they say autocratic leadership is that the leader dominates by force, power, coercion, threats, etc. While directing can have a sometimes-negative reputation, there are times when this style is appropriate. An appropriate time to use a directing style would be in an emergency, such as an emergency department physician providing trauma care. Another less dramatic situation where directing would be an appropriate style would be if a dining room captain was having places set by entry level servers for a banquet of 100 guests.

- Coaching. In the coaching style, leaders continue to define tasks and supervise closely. However, leaders begin to seek ideas, input, and suggestions from followers. Communication is far more two-way in that there is an expected give and take between leader and follower. Coaching is also referred to as consultative.

An application appropriate for a coaching style would include followers who have some relevant experience performing a related task, but might not be fully capable of performing the particular task. More specifically, we may have a group of machinists who have a great deal of experience cutting precision automobile pistons from steel who are now asked to cut a specialized connector using titanium.

- Supporting. In a supporting style, it is appropriate for leaders to pass day-to-day decision making along to followers. Here, the leader facilitates work processes and an outcome, but control of goal achievement lies with the followers, as their responsibility. Communication is very much oriented from followers to the leader. Supporting is often referred to as participative or democratic.

  Applications for a supporting leadership style are many. By definition, we have a situation whereby a follower is capable (high commitment) but may lack the confidence to take charge and go it alone. Specifically, think about a situation such as a long time supervisor of a hotel front desk is offered the position as front desk manager. A supporting style helps allay the follower's doubts in him or herself.

- Delegating. In delegating, the leader is involved in major decisions and problem solving, but otherwise followers are in control. Because followers are in control of work processes and outcomes, the followers invite the leader in when they want his or her involvement. Delegating is often referred to as laissez-faire.

  Delegating style works quite successfully when the follower is an experienced professional doing an excellent job in his or her position. One example would include an experienced golf professional being encouraged to run his or her day-to-day business within a hotel resort. The General Manager is a specialist in business management but not in golf management.

This theory of Situational Leadership suggests several important lessons and points for consideration.

1. Effective leaders are versatile and should be able to provide variable amounts of control and support to their followers based on follower ability.
2. Less experienced followers need more direction. Followers who are more capable need to be encouraged, but do not need or appreciate constant micro managing from their leaders.
3. Leaders, especially in large organizations, cannot possibly (and should not attempt to) run their day-to-day organizations—at some point it becomes physically impossible to do so. Therefore using situational leadership allows a leader to focus his or her attention where it is needed, which makes leadership manageable.
4. The supporting leader involves fellow workers and constituents in the process of making important decisions. This does not mean that the leader acquiesces to the responsibility of making decisions, instead it means that followers aide in making decisions—they have expected and binding input.
5. The coaching, supporting, and delegating environments foster decision-making by lower level management by degree because task and authority have been delegated.
6. Information flows laterally and downward in the coaching, supporting, and delegating organizational structure, whereas the directing leader typically keeps followers in the dark and makes his or her own decisions.
7. Over managing and trying to do too much is a very common pitfall of less experienced leaders. They typically believe that they must try to do it all and do not know how to delegate effectively. Left unchanged, this behavior leads to inefficient management and possibly burnout.
8. While there are situations that favor a directing style over the more participative styles, current trends seem to favor a style, which ideally moves along the continuum toward delegating where possible and or practical.
9. In an ideal, established, and effective work environment, all followers would be trained and educated with high competence and high ability in their jobs, which would allow the leader to use a delegating leadership style.

Assessment and Motivation. Assessment and motivation are inherent in the contingency model; thus, according to this model the leader must possess skills in these areas to be effective. To move a person or a group from M1 to M4 takes leader time, perseverance, and talent. The leader must continuously motivate followers toward established goals, and be able to assess the follower's skill level. Skill levels are viewed relative to where the follower is to where the follower needs to be when the desired competency level is reached. This model is limited in that it should only be employed with one skill at a time. The starting point on the curve corresponds to the follower's maturity, and this point suggests the leadership style to be adopted. For example, a leader's style may be low-task, low-relationship on a particular skill for a follower, and high task, low- relationship style on another skill. Individual skills are emphasized. Using this model, the leader must be able to demonstrate a mix of two behaviors to institute the appropriate style for followers' maturity levels. In short, a leader must be able to adapt and adjust his or her behavior to react to follower readiness levels.

It is assumed the contingency model may also be used for group behavior as well as individual behavior. The group's maturity level would be assessed in much the same manner as individuals, and change in leadership style would be dictated by group maturity level changes. The problem is that individuals mature at different rates; thus, the leader must assess maturity in an aggregate manner for groups. This could lead to problems that this model does not address. Therefore, care must be used if this model is applied to group behavior. Figure 3 provides a graphic detail of a contingency model.

Figure 3. Situational Leadership Contingency Theory

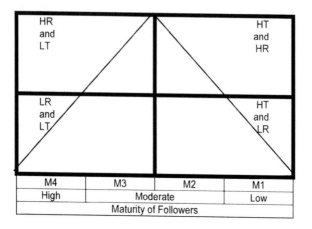

Contingency Model Key:
HR = High Relationship
HT = High Task
LT = Low Task
LR = Low Relationship

LPC Contingency Model (Fiedler). This situational model includes what Fiedler refers to as the group, task, situation (GTS). The group, task, situation includes three elements:
1. Leader/Member Relations--the loyalty, friendliness, and cooperativeness of subordinates toward the leader. It describes the quality of feelings that the group members and the leader have;
2. Position Power--the extent to which the leader's position enables the leader to evaluate and thereby exercise influence over the group in the form of rewards and punishment.
3. Task Structure--the degree to which the group's task, goals, and objectives and other operating procedures are in place and expectations for outcomes are well defined along with an objective plan for assessing goal attainment.
    Fiedler ordered these variables by degree of importance by identifying relations as the most important, task as second, and the leader's power position third. The combination of these factors influences the environment to the point of determining

the most effective style of leadership that the leader should exhibit. Fiedler concluded that the degree to which these factors are present in the environment affects another concept he introduced--situational favorableness.

The favorableness of the situation prescribes the most effective leadership style. Fiedler displayed the favorableness concept in the form:

a) Favorable,

b) Moderately Favorable, and

c) Unfavorable.

Quadrants are used to correspond to groupings with the appropriate leadership style identified. The LPC Contingency Model is diagrammed in Figure 4.

Favorableness is a composite of the three factors. Each variable is considered on a scale (high, low) and then grouped to determine the degree of situation favorableness. By grouping all combinations of the variables, Fiedler categorized the groups into classifications of favorable, moderately favorable, and unfavorable. Fiedler further prescribed a leadership style for each category, which includes two styles in the designated positions within the eight categories:

- Task-oriented style for categories (octaves) 1, 2, 3, and 8.
- Relationship-oriented style for categories 4, 5, 6, and 7.

Fiedler's assumptions:

1. In a favorable situation, the group would complete more tasks, or reach their goals more efficiently with a task-oriented leader. For example, in a favorable situation, the leader/follower relationships are assumed positive and consequently, followers would expect the leader to take charge.

2. In a moderately favorable situation, the relations-oriented leader would be most effective. In a moderately favorable situation, the leader should apply the principles of relationship behavior because relations are poor in three of the four categories. Further, in the category where relations are strong, that category is not supported by the other two categories.

3. In unfavorable conditions, the group would (as in the favorable situation) complete more tasks, or reach their goals more efficiently with a task-oriented leader. Because all categories rate low, the effective leader would apply task behavior to clarify expectations for the group.

With a leader structuring his or her behavior along these lines, the group may be able to realize success and that success may help improve the group/leader relations. While relations (as a category) is the most important variable, it must be supported by the other two variables or the right combination of the other two variables.

As the factors either improve or deteriorate, the variables will change. These changes will likely indicate a change in leadership style. Like the situational model, this model suggests leader adaptability and flexibility. The model indicates that a person may be a successful leader in one situation but not in another. Research supports Fiedler's contention that a leadership style may be indicated; however, one must be cautious of relying on this as a formula for quick leader effectiveness. Since many leaders have a preferred style and therefore often apply their preferred style instead of an indicated/appropriate style, there is a possibility that some leaders will not freely adapt different styles. The degree of leadership effectiveness may be found in the leaders' flexibility in assessing situations, prescribing behaviors, and adapting styles.

Figure 4. LPC Contingency Model
Note: LPC indicates least preferred coworker

	Favorable 1-3			Moderately Favorable 4-7				Unfav
Octant	1	2	3	4	5	6	7	8
Relations	good	good	good	good	poor	poor	poor	poor
Structure	high	high	low	low	high	high	low	low
Power	strong	weak	strong	weak	strong	weak	strong	weak

Elements of Leadership

Power and Leadership. Webster defines power as possession of control, authority, or influence over others. This definition takes on additional meaning when combined with the concept of leadership. Leadership power is based to a great degree of the follower's willingness to be influenced, induced, controlled, and guided by a particular person. One commonly held but mistaken belief, is that a leader is necessarily the person, within a group setting, who holds the highest degree of power and or authority. A person may have power and or authority by virtue of his or her position, but still not be a leader. Also, people are considered leaders because of their rank or title within an organization. However, positions (titles and or ranks) do not possess leadership characteristics, only people possess leadership characteristics. One may expect certain leadership characteristics to be exhibited by people in certain positions, and that a position calls for some expected style of leadership to be anticipated, but a position (title and or rank) itself, of course, does not exhibit leadership.

Leadership power is derived from a follower's willingness to be led. That is not to say that individuals in administrative and managerial positions do not have power, because they do have power. Position power is derived from vested authority and responsibilities and is different from power bestowed by willingness to follow. A person may possess both position power and personal power, maximizing his or her influence. Leadership power is derived from the fact that followers allow themselves to be influenced; thus, merely possessing position power does not make one a leader. Furthermore, power does not create a leader; power is derived from someone being—in action and behavior—a leader.

We will identify and examine several types of power:

Position Power. Chester Barnard developed the Zone of Indifference theory, which posits that followers may allow supervisors, managers, and administrators to exercise control over them as a condition of organizational rank. According to this concept, the follower is willing to be influenced or controlled by the authority vested within a position's bounds, but may or may not be willing to be influenced beyond the position's vested authority. The amount of position power that a person inherits, because of the power vested in the position, influences how much control the person has over a group.

Representation Power. The leader is usually given the power to represent a group internally and or externally. The leader may be the representative for the missions, goals, and operations of the group and may communicate the purpose and intent of group actions to entities external to the group. Internally, the leader may occupy any position; the consistent factor is that group members look to the leader to represent their interests.

Purpose Power. The concept of purpose power suggests that mission or purpose of the group takes priority over the desires of any single individual or individuals. Therefore, leader actions that are perceived as group goal directed and actions that perpetuate group purpose are considered more important than special interests that arise. Group purpose is apparent in the leader, so the group, as long as they represent the group's purpose and intent, accepts his or her actions.

Legitimate Power. A legitimate power base can be exercised through the acquisition of formal authority, title, and or position. Legitimate power is also enforced by organizational edict, the existence of an organizational chart delineating reporting relationships, and a willingness of others to recognize and accept that source.

Reward Power. Influencing the behavior of another by the benefit of a reward can result in power for the benefactor. The reward must be perceived to be of value to the recipient in order to alter performance. In addition to pay, promotion, and prestige, rewards may include praise, publicity, respect, favorable working conditions or scheduling, and other such considerations perceived as desirable by the recipient.

Coercive Power. Coercive power is the opposite of reward power. One possesses power in this mode if the leader has the ability to punish or withhold rewards for non-performance in a prescribed manner. Punishment or withholding rewards includes denial of raises, demotion, unfavorable transfer, or other actions that are deemed undesirable by the recipient. Coercive power is not always as overt as other forms of power. However, a person under the influence of another must perceive that the supervisor has the capability and authority to use coercive power.

Personal Power. Beyond power being granted to a leader administratively, effective leaders use their personalities to help influence subordinates. Leaders may have magnetic personalities; people are naturally and positively drawn to them. This is not always true, however, as some leaders may not be liked, but are still perceived as having personal qualities that are worth emulating. Leaders can use this personality attraction as a power of presence to influence the group. Minimally, a leader is perceived as one who has the qualities to get the job accomplished. The group's collective feelings concerning the leader's positive qualities (whether they like the leader or not) give the leader personality power.

Influence Power. If a group perceives a person as their leader, this person has inherent influence within the group. The leader usually has the power to influence policy, operations, and the general group climate. The leader is usually a key person in establishing important work relationships and how people interact to accomplish group missions.

Expert Power. If one is judged as possessing more knowledge or skill, he or she may influence others who have correspondingly less knowledge or skill. The importance of this form of power is easily discernible in a superior-subordinate relationship and either person can enhance his position of power by using it.

Referent Power. Referent power may exist when a person is liked, admired, or respected because of personality traits or skills that another finds desirable. The person who holds this power over another, may or may not be conscious of such influence. People like to identify with those they perceive as winners.

Power may be used in many ways, but it is important to realize that position power is limited by the boundaries of the position's authority. Leadership power, by definition, is power the group gives the leader. Followers perceive the leader will use the power to move the group in a desired direction. On occasion, the leader may be allowed to go beyond position bounds because leadership power expands the zone of influence of the leader. Leadership power is accepted as goal directed and it is not likely that a group would continue to support a leader who is perceived as detrimental to that group's purpose. Therefore, leadership power is bestowed on the leader, and perceived by group members as being goal oriented.

Current leadership concepts do not recognize brute force as a leadership element, but rather that leadership power is a form of influence and inducement. Therefore, the difference between position power and leadership power is one of -follower perception. Position power is accepted by followers because it is perceived as the authority in a position. Leadership power is accepted because followers perceive the use of power as promoting group goals, purpose, and values. There is willingness of followers to submit to leadership power because of an overriding commitment to group values. The difference in these types of power may be subtle, but substantial.

Power is recognized as a leadership element, but it can easily be misinterpreted. Power is not leadership, but leaders have power. Power is manifest in the leader's actions to achieve group goals. Position power may be easily misinterpreted as leadership power because people frequently use their positions in an influential manner. However, not all types of influence are necessarily leadership influence. The test to determine if power is vested in leadership can be determined by answers to the following questions:

1. Do followers express a willingness to recognize power beyond influence inherent in a position?, and
2. Is the leader's power used to influence action to realize group goals?

Group Behavior

Groups. Becoming familiar with group dynamics is important in understanding the nature of leadership. A group, in a context of leadership, has a special meaning; it is not simply a gathering of people, but rather a gathering of people who have come together for a specific reason, intent, or purpose and are bound by certain moral and or philosophical beliefs and or values. In studying leadership, it is important to note and understand some group characteristics and the manner in which groups take action.

Group actions can be categorized in three fundamental ways:

1. Interacting. Interacting groups are those in which the product outcome involves a group effort and the members work interdependently with one another.
2. Co-acting. Co-acting groups are those in which the members work independently of one another.
3. Counteracting. Counteracting groups are those in which members compete with one another.

When these three classifications are applied to leadership theory, we discover the following relationships:

- The Fiedler Situational Model applies to groups in which individuals within the groups are interacting and not to groups in which members either work independently or compete within the group.
- Hersey and Blanchard's Contingency model applies to all three classifications of groups and may be applied to individuals.
- The Grid Approach is one that is geared to individual leader behavior. Therefore, groups and their corresponding work would not be considered within the boundaries of this approach.

The study of group dynamics is necessary for serious students of leadership, because leadership, by definition, takes place within a group setting. Group dynamics goes beyond mere group classifications and delves into the inter-workings of various group types.

Time: A Leadership Variable

Likert's Time-Lag Concept. Rensis Likert's concept stresses group performance and environmental climate as the primary forces that produce results (outcomes). The importance of this concept lies within its recognition that leader actions do not directly affect results. Instead, leader actions affect results indirectly. Likert suggests that there is a time lapse between leader action and results.

Likert identifies three concepts to support his hypothesis:

1. Causal variables. Causal variables are elements that are under the control of the leader and include issues such as philosophy, structure of the organization, policies, rules, regulations, leader behavior, and the like.

2. Intervening variables. Intervening variables are those elements that are affected by causal variables. They include issues such as climate of the organization, attitudes of the employees, perceptions, and politics among group members, etc.

3. End-result variables. End-result variables can also be described as the product or outcome. Likert posits that end-results are the product of the first two variables (causal and intervening variables) and that the cause/effect relationship between the first two variables creates a natural flow to produce the third variable, end-results. For example, in a school setting, end-result variables might include test scores, rate of attendance, percentage of college-bound students as compared to the total school population, teacher turnover rate, etc.

This model is referred to as time lag, because, in most cases results are not immediately realized when leader action is taken and time becomes a variable that effects realization of goals and objectives. Most complex organizations have goals that are realized longitudinally across time. Consequently, the benefit of a leader's action taken today may take years to be fully realized. The Likert model takes into consideration the time element involved in fully realizing the effect of leader actions. That is, the affect that leader actions have on causal and intervening variables on end-result variables.

An example of the time lag concept: A college dean maintains relatively high morale and good relations with professors, but the college's student test scores fall far below the national average. The university president is concerned about the test scores and eventually terminates the dean. The president hires a hard-nosed dean to get the test scores in this particular college back up to the national average.

The new dean raises the test scores but is so tough on the professors that he/she has caused half of the faculty to leave the college. The test scores are up, but the morale of the faculty is down. In the end faculty production will drop which will cause declining test scores.

Between the time of the test scores going up for the hard-nosed dean and then going down again, pressure has been placed on the president, and as a result the hard-nosed dean is fired, and the president hires another dean who can get along with the college faculty. This cycle may continue indefinitely, revealing the president's actions and over time, affects the college climate. This ultimately affects the end-results sought by the university. This example provides a clear picture of the time lag effect. One cannot always accurately judge the effect of a leader's actions at the time that they occur. The proper criterion for judging a leader's actions is the long-term effect that actions have on end-results.

Figure 5. Time Lag Model

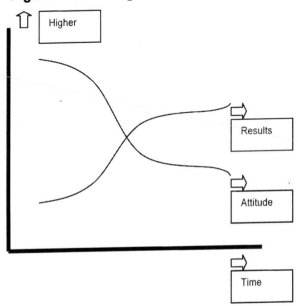

Philosophy and Style

Theory X and Theory Y. Rather than a theory on leadership, Theory X and Theory Y is a philosophy as to how people view other human beings. This theory is significant because how leaders relate to others is a critical element in predicting leader behavior. The value of Theory X and Theory Y comes in realizing that it places emphasis on the particular leader's attitudes. A leader's attitude about people in general, is a key in the development of leader-follower relations.

Theory X. The assumptions:
1. The average person has an inherent dislike for work and will avoid it if possible;
2. Most people must be coerced, controlled, directed, or threatened with punishment to get them to exert adequate effort toward the achievement of organizational objectives; and
3. The average person prefers direction, wishes to avoid responsibility, has relatively little ambition, and wants security above all else.

Theory Y. The assumptions:
1. The expenditure of physical and mental effort in work is as natural as play, as long as it is satisfying;
2. People will exercise self-direction and self-control toward an organization's goals if they are committed to the goals;
3. Commitment to objectives is a function of rewards associated with their achievement; The most effective rewards are satisfaction of ego and self-actualization;
4. The average person learns, given favorable conditions, to not accept and seek responsibility. Avoidance of responsibility and emphasis on security are learned and not inherited characteristics; and
5. Creativity, ingenuity, and imagination are widespread among people.

All people like to be treated with dignity and respect. Effective leaders should review Theory X and Theory Y assumptions and ensure that they have or develop Theory Y philosophies. For Theory X leaders, especially in a setting that deals directly with people, time has come and gone. It is likely that leaders with this predominate style will not be successful in people-oriented environments.

Theory Z. Theory X and Theory Y assume that a leader's general outlook toward people will help determine the leadership style that a leader will tend to adopt. Another theory that makes a similar assumption is Theory Z, which came into prominence during the 1970s. Theory Z is the direct opposite of a bureaucratic philosophy of management and counters the view that leadership must be a behavioral continuum. Theory Z's philosophy implies trust in the judgment of people and embraces group members' opinions to help influence group actions.

Application of Theory Z stresses upward mobility for all group members with skill specialization so that group members can become competent in specific areas. However, after becoming a competent specialist in one area, group members are encouraged to progress to other tasks, which will challenge their existing skills and intellect, thereby encouraging group members to view education and training as a never-ending and key element of career and personal development.

Position security is another mainstay of Theory Z; providing group members with the opportunity to work in confidence while knowing their positions will not be threatened. Theory Z also encourages an attitude of greater cooperative effort between and among group members and group leaders, allowing leaders to obtain firsthand information about group activities and making followers feel they are part of the leadership team.

The leadership philosophy in many organizations during the 1900s in the United States was the opposite of Theory Z. One of the main influences in the United States was the work of Max Weber and the development of bureaucratic structure. Weber's philosophy of management can be observed throughout federal, state, and local government, the military, and other organizations. The bureaucratic philosophy stresses chain of command, span of control, policies, regulations, and rank. It is obvious that organizational structures have influenced how leaders have developed and expressed their leadership styles. Current trends in the 2000s appear to be shifting toward Theory Z, as reflected in the manner in which organizations are operated.

Evaluation

Success and Effectiveness. There is a difference between being an effective leader and being a successful leader. Leadership that produces desired results may be termed successful, but not necessarily effective. A leader can be successful without being effective, but cannot be effective without being successful.

Successful leadership results in intended group behavior, but in the long-run success alone may not produce desired results. One could achieve all the goals set forth for a group and still not be considered effective. The effective leader will motivate the follower toward continued success and instill in the follower the desire to strive for future goals. The non-effective leader may accomplish immediate goals, but not motivate the followers for future activity. The effective leader will take into consideration follower feelings and desires, and attempt to satisfy the followers' personal needs as well as accomplishing group goals. Effectiveness is a process; the result is success and motivated followers.

Addressing follower satisfaction is a primary element in developing an effective leadership style. Knowing what satisfies a particular follower may vary from group to group, but the astute leader will learn the satisfying environmental elements as well as the dissatisfying environmental elements. The effective leader will seek to minimize the latter while maximizing the former. The desired result for the leader is successful accomplishment of goals, as well as a satisfied and motivated work group. Figure 6 illustrates an example of effectiveness as it relates to success.

Figure 6. Effective and Non-Effective Success

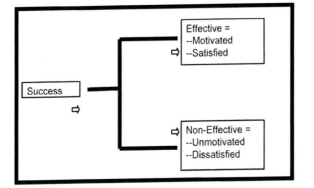

A leader's behavior is particularly difficult to assess since, to be considered effective, the leader must be both able and willing to lead; the followers must be both able and willing to follow. A diagram of willing and able is illustrated in Figure 7. There are four combinations (of leader and follower) for failure and only one combination (of leader and follower) for success. This being illustrated, is it reasonable to conclude that it is four times as easy to fail as to succeed when leading people? Or for that matter, is it four times as easy to fail anytime one deals with people? Perhaps that is not the discrete conclusion to draw from this line of reasoning, but almost anyone who has been in a position of dealing with groups will admit that it is difficult to be successful. The leader's responsibility when dealing with people is to turn the failure situations into the success situations by creating willing and able scenarios for all involved.

Three criteria of leader effectiveness that are used as a base for study:

1. Group satisfaction,
2. Group productivity, and
3. Group performance.

In many cases, these criteria are judged by questionnaires administered to the group under study. However, there are several different ways by which to judge effectiveness. The concept of effectiveness in leadership has much to do with motivation of followers. The concept of effectiveness is central to the study of leadership.

Figure 7. Five Leadership Effectiveness Combinations

	Behavior Characteristics		Effectiveness Outcome	
1.	**Follower is:**	**Leader is:**	Failure	Success
	Willing to be led	Willing to lead	☑	
	Able to be led	**(Unable to lead)**		

	Behavior Characteristics		Effectiveness Outcome	
2.	**Follower is:**	**Leader is:**	Failure	Success
	Willing to be led	**(Unwilling to lead)**	☑	
	Able to be led	Able to lead		

	Behavior Characteristics		Effectiveness Outcome	
3.	**Follower is:**	**Leader is:**	Failure	Success
	(Unwilling to be led)	Willing to lead	☑	
	Able to be led	Able to lead		

	Behavior Characteristics		Effectiveness Outcome	
4.	**Follower is:**	**Leader is:**	Failure	Success
	Willing to be led	Willing to lead	☑	
	(Unable to be led)	Able to lead		

	Behavior Characteristics		Effectiveness Outcome	
5.	**Follower is:**	**Leader is:**	Failure	Success
	Willing to be led	Willing to lead		☑
	Able to be led	Able to lead		

Leadership Skill

Many of the current approaches to leadership have focused on behavioral elements. Studies of leader behavior have been thought to reveal and or suggest success and effectiveness patterns. Analysis of specific situations has provided insight to the type of leader behavior, which is thought to be most effective for a particular situation. Another approach to leadership has been to identify skills that when executed successfully, yield effective leadership. With this approach, the leader exhibits certain skills, and is rated on his or her successful execution. The major emphasis of this line of thought is on teaching skills of how to become a leader. It is assumed that if someone can be taught appropriate skills that he or she will become an effective leader.

This approach highlights a philosophical argument: Is leadership an art or a science? The answer to this question is probably both. The answer lies somewhere in a gray area, as leadership is both an art and a science. The degree of whether art or science depends on personal interpretation and, perhaps, application. It is important to note that the skills approach is not all-inclusive. Competence in certain skills does not necessarily guarantee leadership success. Necessary skills in one situation may not be a requirement in another situation. Thus, to determine the skills necessary for success, one needs to analyze carefully the specific leadership situation in question.

Certainly, some group of skills is necessary for one to become a competent, successful, and effective leader. However, the type of skills and degree of expertise depends on the environment—often referred to as the situation. Assessing skills required for effective leadership without analyzing the environment is tricky. For example, an engineering environment would require demonstration of different skills than a social-work environment. There may be leadership skills common to both environments, such as effective communication. However, there are skills unique to both environments, which require their own type and degree of competency. The student of leadership should be careful not to view execution of skills as leadership itself. The act of executing skills does not equate to leadership, but execution of skills may be necessary to be a leader in a particular situation.

Execution of skills involves a process that affects the perception of leader effectiveness. Therefore, it would be easy to confuse the process of executing a skill with leadership when really it is the effectiveness of executing the skill, which is being judged. There is a difference between executing a skill and effective leadership. Although the two may be related, short-term execution should not be judged as effective leadership. Effective leadership and execution of skills should be judged across different parameters.

The skills approach typically describes the necessary skills a person must competently demonstrate to be a successful leader. On the other hand, behavioral approaches typically prescribe behaviors the leader must exhibit to be effective. Many of the theories covered in this chapter are related either directly or indirectly to behavioral theories. Some theories have considered follower readiness and the general climate that exists between leader and follower.

In review, all of the topics that have been covered are important to the study of leadership and all impact leadership. It is advisable to become familiar with several approaches to leadership to obtain a broad understanding of this concept.

Chapter 02:

Motivation

Introduction

Chapter two examines motivation. Motivation is an integral element of leadership, and is included as a major section in the majority of leadership texts. This chapter provides a descriptive narrative of the subject and provides insight into many of the current theories of motivation. Here is a brief rundown of the theories of motivation that are covered:

Expectancy Theory is the first to be covered in this chapter. It presents a process model of how people are motivated. The drive of Expectancy Theory is that people have choices to make, and for their effort expended, people expect results. Several questions are addressed within this theory:

- What do we perceive as the pay-off for our efforts?
- What is it that drives us?
- Why do we choose the goals we choose?

These are some questions that Expectancy Theory explores. Expectancy Theory is a psychological theory that places the individual in the position of choosing between or among values.

Path Goal Theory emphasizes the leader and stresses how a leader must recognize the needs of the follower while recognizing the elements in the environment that may keep the follower from accomplishing established goals. Path Goal Theory posits that it is the responsibility of the leader to remove external obstacles that would hinder the follower in accomplishing his or her goals.

Maslow's Hierarchy of Needs delineates personal needs and orders them sequentially into priorities of likely fulfillment. This theory provides a framework in which a continuum of motivational factors is considered in the priority of how they may be satisfied.

Herberg's Two-Factor Theory considers two sets of factors--maintenance factors and motivation factors. Maintenance factors do not motivate, but they help keep employees from being dissatisfied. This theory proposes that if a person is dissatisfied then he or she is not capable of being motivated.

Background

Motivation. Motivation in organizations and institutions over the past 100 years has been handled predominantly from a negative perspective. Followers have been largely motivated with words that go something like this:

If you do not do (insert some task or a project that the leader wants done here), then (insert some negative outcome or punishment here) will happen. Some refer to this method as motivation by fear or intimidation. Whatever the case, it is certainly an example of negatively oriented motivation. Negative motivation may be the most often-used method, but it is not always the case and is rarely the preferred method.

In many instances, effective leaders instinctively know that each follower is different and that not all individuals are motivated by the same things. Moreover, they realize that not all people can be treated effectively in exactly the same manner. However, all people should always be treated with both dignity and respect. Leaders who hold this view tend to make an effort to know their followers and know why and how each person is different. These leaders do not stress the sameness of followers; instead, they notice individual qualities. Astute leaders use these differences to their advantage in dealing with followers. Many theories stress the importance of an individual in motivation and thereby address factors that cause people to take certain actions over others.

The term drive is often used in psychological circles to describe the amount of energy focused and channeled toward accomplishment of a particular objective. The direction and intensity of a person's motivation are influenced by two factors:
1. A person's perceptions of him or her self (intrinsic) and
2. A person's perception of the world external to him or her self (extrinsic).

A person's perception of how well he or she can perform and the external forces acting on the individual to either aid or hinder performance will influence:
1. Whether the individual will or will not take action and
2. The amount of energy that will be exerted toward the action.

In considering motivation, one should realize that any environment involving people deals with varying degrees of uncertainty. One cannot always accurately assess how others will react to particular leader behaviors.

For example, an administrator praises John for a job well done. Afterward, John demonstrates a 10 percent increase in work output. The leader uses the same technique with Ken only to observe a corresponding decline in Ken's work. Notice that identical leader behavior resulted in two distinctly different responses. Later, the same leader praises John and gets another increase in performance. Now the leader criticizes Ken and observes a corresponding increase in Ken's work. A reverse effect is observed. This illustrates that individual followers may react the same to different leader behavior. This may be due to differences in individual preferences or it may be due to differences in perception by the individuals themselves.

This text will cover several theories on the subject of motivation. These theories attempt to explain why people act as they do. Some of these theories address issues that motivate others and some address the process of motivating others. Inferences are made concerning group behavior from conclusions drawn about individual behavior. These inferences are used to help explain how motivational factors affect groups. Trying to draw inferences from individual behavior and to predict or prescribe group behavior can be problematic. To think that motivational factors of individuals are also descriptive of a particular group's motivational climate is not valid reasoning. The approach that we will present in this chapter is primarily focused on individuals, with the hope that one can gain some understanding about group actions, as well. The study of these motivation theories will provide insight into the nature of motivation and allow one to use this information to gain an understanding of peoples' actions.

One of the primary tasks of any leader is to try to help motivate followers, both individually and collectively. Knowing what prompts a follower to action can help provide the leader with the tools necessary to accomplish group tasks and goals.

Many current theories treat motivation as a process that begins with some unsatisfied need. A need produces tension, which in turn stimulates a level of drive within the individual. Drive leads to a search for appropriate behavior to achieve the goal and thereby to satisfy the need. If the need is satisfied, then the tension is thereby relieved.

Figure 8. Seven Steps of Motivation

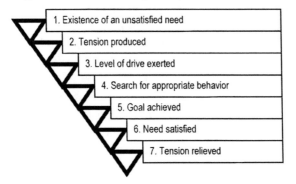

1. Existence of an unsatisfied need
2. Tension produced
3. Level of drive exerted
4. Search for appropriate behavior
5. Goal achieved
6. Need satisfied
7. Tension relieved

Expectancy Theory

Expectancy theory evolved around the process illustrated in Figure 8. Three assumptions of expectancy theory:

1. People do not just respond to events after they occur; they anticipate or expect that things will occur and that certain behaviors in response to those events will probably produce predictable consequences;
2. People usually confront possible alternative behaviors in rational manners, and
3. Over time, people learn to predict likely consequences and therefore modify their behavior in a way that desired results could possibly be achieved.

The constructs that follow help provide an understanding of motivation in terms of expectancy:

Valence. Valence refers to the degree of preference that one has for a potential outcome. Valence can be either positive or negative. Different people will assign different values to items and issues such as income, working conditions, status, or security. Valence helps define the parameters of what an individual wants and or expects from a job.

Outcome. Outcome is the consequence, product, or result of one's behavior.

Action. Action is open, observable, and obvious behavior. Action entails physical movement as well as cognitive content and emotional tone. Expectancy theory assumes a range of behavior is available to and applicable by each individual.

Expectancy. Expectancy is the belief that some particular behavior will likely result in a predictable, first-level outcome.

First level outcome. First level outcome is the direct or immediate consequence of one's behavior.

Second level outcome. Second level outcome refers to the personal impact that the first level outcome has on a particular individual. A first level outcome may affect something else in the life of the individual. For example, more productive work on the job (action) may produce better pay (first level outcome), which may yield a better lifestyle for the worker (second level outcome). Better lifestyle is a second level outcome that occurred directly because of the first level outcome.

Instrumental Effect. Instrumental effect refers to a correlation between the first level outcome and the second level outcome. It is an individual's perception as to how strongly the initial outcome (first level outcome) will affect other outcomes (second level and subsequent outcomes).

Figure 9. Motivation as a Form of Expectancy

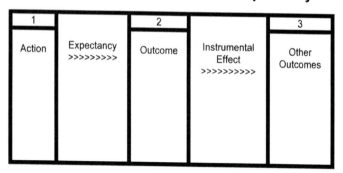

A direct outcome is desirable or undesirable to the extent that it is perceived to relate to indirect outcomes that are desirable or undesirable. A direct outcome takes on valence as it is perceived to be instrumental in attaining desired indirect outcomes and or avoiding unpleasant indirect outcomes.

Expectancy theory is a psychological theory that places the individual in the position of choosing among values. It is based on the assumption that all human behavior can be regarded as the result of a state of internal tension which serves as a drive for action. It is drive that produces the energy to act. Expectancy theory is a descriptive model of how individuals act relative to their perception of environmental stimulus.

One major force within an individual is his or her perception concerning their ability to act. A second major force is the perceived consequence of action taken. These two forces are major factors in determining whether an individual will take action, and the degree of energy the individual will exert toward the action. Expectancy theory helps explain the process of how individuals are motivated and the factors present when an individual is motivated. Understanding the motivational process will help leaders identify ways to motivate individuals. It is incumbent on the leader to recognize what followers value— the elements that cause internal tension. It is also important for the leader to recognize how followers perceive their ability to act. Confidence is a major factor in successful completion of activities.

Path-Goal Theory. R.J. House's Path-Goal Theory is one example of Expectancy Theory. This theory hypothesizes that if a follower clearly understands the path to take to reach a desired goal, and explicitly understands the rewards that will be received if he or she is successful, then that person will be motivated to choose the appropriate path that leads to the rewards that best suit his or her wants and needs. An individual can expect certain outcomes from actions because the various paths to those outcomes have been clearly identified. The individual is motivated by clearly understanding the amount of energy (drive) needed to achieve a particular outcome. An individual is also motivated to achieve a particular outcome if the path has been cleared of as many possible obstacles as can be anticipated.

According to Path-Goal Theory, the primary function of the leader then becomes one of a facilitator in removing obstacles from the path of followers so that desired outcomes may become realized. The leader should provide skill training for the follower to accomplish desired goals, and identify the necessary amount of effort that will be required to accomplish an outcome. The leader should point out the reward for successful accomplishment, and help show the follower the way to go about successful accomplishment. House is quick to make leaders and followers aware that there is no guarantee of success even if the follower is aware of the means of reaching his or her goals and even if most obstacles are removed from the follower's path. A major portion of responsibility for success lies with the follower. The follower must value (have valence for) the goal enough to take the necessary action (drive) to fulfill the goal.

House and Dressler provide six suggestions for implementing Path-Goal Theory:

1. Recognize and arouse the follower's need for outcomes over which the leader has some control;
2. Increase personal payoffs to followers for successful goal attainment;
3. Make the path to payoff easier to obtain by offering coaching, directing, and other forms of mentoring;
4. Help followers clarify expectations in terms of objective terms (discrete metrics which can either be timed and or counted);

5. Reduce frustrating barriers; and
6. Increase the opportunity for personal satisfaction contingent upon effective performance as evaluated in terms of objective measures.

If these guidelines are implemented, the result should be a significantly higher percentage of followers who are motivated and directed. Path-Goal Theory places the follower at the front of the focus—the follower successfully completes tasks to achieve goals, while the leader provides the guidance and direction.

It is necessary for the leader to understand the individual follower's wants and needs and also the group's wants and needs. The leader must know the task accomplishments that are necessary for the follower to realize success. This implies that the leader must understand the environment and have empathy for the follower's goals. Leaders using any leadership style needs:

1. Know and understand themselves;
2. Understand the external environment in which they are working; and
3. Know and understand their followers.

Knowledge of one's strengths and limitations, and knowing the followers' characteristics are basic issues for practical application of Motivation Theory.

When the path (means for accomplishing a goal) is clear to followers, research shows that some followers do not respond well to further path clarification. This may help explain why many people resent close monitoring and or micromanaging. These types of people believe that they are professional, know their jobs, know what is expected of them, and can operate independently. They prefer a style whereby a leader provides the structure for getting the goal achieved and then allows the follower to execute the plan. Research efforts in the area of motivation have been contradictory in its findings. However, this can be expected since motivation deals with prescribing, predicting, and explaining human behavior.

Figure 10. Path-Goal Theory as Financial Security or Peer Recognition

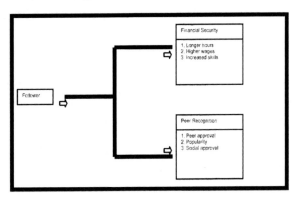

The follower will choose among the paths that they perceive fulfill their needs. This process helps explain some of the issues that motivate people. It does not attempt to either define or otherwise explain the nature of motivation, it simply attempts to identify some elements that cause a person to take action. If given a choice, which would you choose, peer recognition or financial security? Of course, it is not always a matter of simply choosing, it is often a matter of simultaneously working on several paths to achieve desired goals.

The House approach suggests that there is a more or less general pattern to one's actions. These patterns provide insight into a follower's behavior and can help a leader establish a meaningful leadership plan (rewards, task, goals, and expectations). It is difficult to judge how much value (utility) a person may place on any specific goal, especially when involved in complex environments. However, one primary leader task is to assess what motivates followers and to use this information to achieve optimal follower performance.

Maslow' s Hierarchy of Needs

Maslow's theory is one that delineates personal needs and orders them in priorities of likely fulfillment. This theory is based on four assumptions:

1. A need that has already been satisfied is not a motivational factor.
2. Needs of an individual are complex; nothing is as neat as a hierarchy is and one is subject to a variety of needs.
3. One will tend to be motivated toward higher order needs once the lower-level needs are met.
4. Higher-level needs may be met but there are relatively few ways in which to satisfy lower-level needs.

This theory provides a framework in which to conceptualize what motivates individuals. Figure 11 shows the process that illustrates this theory.

Figure 11. Maslow's Hierarchy of Needs

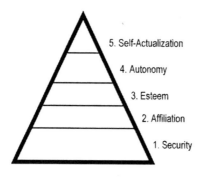

In our society, we typically assume that most followers' basic needs are being met, which allows us to concentrate effort on higher order needs, such as self-actualization. In reality, basic needs being met may or may not be a valid assumption.

Herzberg's Two-Factor Theory.

Another motivation theory is the Herzberg's Two-Factor Theory. The Two-Factor Theory is different from the Maslow

Theory in that Herzberg posits that motivation cannot be sufficiently explained in terms of a hierarchy alone. Instead, he theorized that motivation is composed of two distinct factors, which he referred to as being either motivational or maintenance.

Herzberg's primary assumptions:

1. Maintenance factors
   a. Must be sufficiently present in order for motivational factors to come into play.
   b. When not sufficiently present, conditions can be created that can block motivation and lead to dissatisfaction.
2. Motivational factors
   a. Lead to satisfaction.

Maintenance factors are not motivational. Instead, they help keep individuals from being dissatisfied. In order for one to be motivated, a follower must derive a certain degree of satisfaction from his or her effort.

According to Herzberg, it is the task of the leader to eliminate or mitigate sources of dissatisfaction for individuals. For example, if a group of workers is to be motivated, then that group must perceive that their environment is significantly free of conditions that Herzberg labeled as dissatisfiers.

Maintenance factors include salary, benefits, working conditions, and other such elements. Herzberg concluded that motivation does not appear to come from maintenance factors, but from other factors. He concluded the factors that incubate motivation include recognition, job challenge, achievement, responsibility, advancement, and promotion.

Historically, researchers had suggested that the opposite of job satisfaction was job dissatisfaction, which sounded logical. And, further, that if the dissatisfaction could be eliminated from work, the job would become both satisfying and motivational. Herzberg disagreed, writing that the opposite of dissatisfaction is not satisfaction. By eliminating sources of dissatisfaction one might reduce the dissatisfaction of a worker, but this does not mean that the worker will somehow become motivated or find job satisfaction.

Like Maslow, Herzberg made fundamental assumptions about this theory:

1. Individuals do not simply respond to events after they occur. Instead, they are highly proactive in trying to shape their events and influence situations, and are thereby proactive.
2. Individuals usually consider alternative behaviors and their possible consequences in a more-or-less rational manner.
3. Through experience, individuals learn to anticipate (forecast) likely outcomes of alternative behaviors in dealing with events and, because of this learning, modify their responses toward positive outcomes.

Figure 12 lists maintenance and motivating factors that may be found in a typical workplace.

Figure 12. Herzberg's Two-Factor Motivational Theory: Motivating Factors and Maintenance Factors

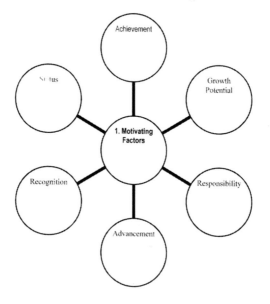

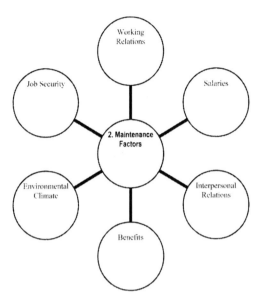

Motivating Factors. There is a limited number of actions that a leader can take to motivate followers. The first action, however, should be for the leader to examine the work environment to identify dissatisfiers. This analysis should then be operationalized with a goal of reducing or eliminating dissatisfiers where possible. It is likely that not all dissatisfiers can be effectively eliminated. However, the demonstration of willingness on the leader's part to act on behalf of the group members typically will positively enhance the leader's image among group members. If the leader evidences a caring attitude, an atmosphere of confidence typically develops toward the leader.

After eliminating elements from the environment that keep people from being motivated, the leader must address the notion of actually motivating followers. To attain this, the leader must determine what it is that his or her followers value and or otherwise care about. In order to do this the leader needs to understand the wants and desires of each group member. This can be quite difficult, but the leader should make a concerted effort to determine wants and needs to help ensure that each individual is being accommodated in such a way as to allow followers to realize their maximum potential.

Maintenance Factors. Application of Herzberg's theory suggests that overall group feelings are a critical element in analyzing the efficacy of maintenance factors. The leader should ensure that dissatisfiers in this category are significantly reduced so that followers will feel compelled to participate in group goals. To the extent possible, group members should share positive feelings overall about interpersonal relations, working relations, salaries, benefits, the environmental climate, and their collective job security.

Chapter 03:

Leader Values, Behavior, and Culture

Introduction

The fundamental idea presented in this chapter is that a leader's values affect his or her enacted behavior, which in turn greatly influences the organization at a level that the leader exerts influence. Therefore, a department head's behavior will affect the culture of individuals, groups, and teams within that particular department. And, as a leader moves up within an organization, his or her behavior naturally affects an increasing number of individuals', groups', and teams' culture.

Values are attitudes about what is correct and incorrect, fair and unfair, honorable and dishonorable (Yukl). Examples of values include fairness, integrity, trustworthiness, courtesy, and support. Values are salient because they influence leader choices, awareness, and behavior, which, in turn influence and shape the work place culture. Leader values and their consequential behavior play an important part in shaping organizations.

The concept of leader behavior suggests that managers may use certain behavior in order to contend with the varying demands of their positions.

Organizational culture (also referred to as corporate culture) has received varying degrees of attention over the years. It first became popular in Barnard's (1938) research into the functions of executives setting the tone for the organization. It underwent a resurgence in popularity in the '90s as organizations began to search for cultures that foster an environment for teams, particularly self-managed teams (Mohrman & Mohrman).

Background

The Relationship Between Values and Behavior

Values are important because they influence leader preferences, perceptions, and behavior, which, in turn influence and shape the work place.

Values are fundamental convictions that a certain mode of behavior or end result state is preferable to a converse mode or end result existence (Rokeach). Values have nested within them an element of judgment in that they are a reflection of an individual's or group's belief about what is right, desirable, or good. Values have attributes regarding content and attributes that regulate intensity. The content attribute states that some behavior or end result is desirable. The intensity attribute states the importance of such behavior or end state. By ranking values by intensity, an idea of a person's individual or work group's value system can be obtained (Bales & Cohen).

Values are important to the study of leadership and organizational culture because they help establish a foundation for the understanding of attitudes and motivation and because they influence perceptions, attitudes, and behavior (Connor & Becker). Individuals enter organizations with interpretations and ideas of what should and should not be. Furthermore, such interpretations imply that some behavior or end states are preferable to others. As a result, individuals' value systems may be incongruent with those of the organization. With an increasing demand by consumers for a higher level and quality of service (Cline; Coyle & Dale; Zeithaml, Parasuraman, & Berry), the effect of values on employee organizational culture becomes a key issue to help ensure that individual value systems are aligned with those of the employing organization's staff, in order to meet such demand.

A review of the literature substantiates Bales' work in integrating interpersonal behavior and values. Many researchers treat behavior as phenomena characteristic of developing lists of traits. Others, such as McDougall, and Lewin, theorize that behavior is part of a higher-order system. In this higher-order system, values are considered more complex than behavior and the product of multiple filters.

McClelland attests that values guide interpersonal behavior, and states that they are best obtained from questionnaires and non-obtrusive observational methods. Triandis believes that values are a critical determinant of social behavior. Elizur et al. assert that values motivate goal-directed behavior. Hofstede suggests that values determine the meanings of people's behavior.

Kluckhohn and Strodtbeck offer, from an anthropological perspective, their definition of value orientations as being complex, rank-ordered principles developing from cognitive, affective, and directive elements. And, such influences provide order and direction for the ever-changing situations.

Feather contends that individual values, as they relate to behavior and social interaction, were largely ignored by psychologists in favor of behaviorism, personality theories, and group dynamics.

Bales suggests that behavior is observed. And, that once observed, certain evaluations are placed on such behavior. The evaluations inform a behavioral response to the original initiated act. These evaluations can be treated as sets of values held by both the observer and the person being observed. Moreover, Bales contends that values' primary focus is the evaluation tool for the behavior of the self and others in interaction. Thus, values and behavior are closely intertwined.

Values and Culture

Shared values are a vital component of organizational culture. Shared values are not easily observable, even though most organizational members are aware of and can describe them (Nahavandi & Malekzadeh). They include values and beliefs that are shared among an organization's members about what is important, such as what the organization stands for, what the organization is about, and what the organization values in their employees.

Employee Culture

A third concept of leadership inquiry examined was that of organizational culture (also referred to as corporate culture).

Organizational culture has received varying degrees of attention over the years. It became popular in Barnard's research into the functions of executives—that of setting the tone for the organization, and again in the 1990s as organizations began to search for cultures that support and integrate self-managed teams (Mohrman & Mohrman).

According to Smircich, organizational culture can be defined as a fairly stable set of assumptions, shared meanings, and values that form a framework for action. Ott offers another conception of culture as shared values, beliefs, assumptions, perceptions, norms, artifacts, and patterns of behavior. Culture includes jargon and slang, humor and jokes, and other such forms (Trice & Beyer). It can also include strong ideologies (Hyde). Strong ideologies make an organization conservative, since actions and decisions are made within a particular ideological framework. Schein defines organizational culture as shared assumptions and beliefs about the world, the nature of time and space, human nature, and relationships. Schein distinguishes between underlying beliefs (which may be unconscious) and espoused values, which may or may not be consistent with these beliefs. However, Schein found that espoused values do not accurately reflect the culture when they are inconsistent with underlying beliefs.

Hall states that underlying beliefs representing the culture of an organization are responses to problems of adaptation to the environment and internal integration. The primary external problems are the vision and mission, goals and objectives, and evaluation methods. Solving problems of internal integration include determining organization membership, issues of status and power, rewards and punishment, and agreement about the meaning of buzzwords and symbols (Hall).

A major function of organizational culture, therefore, is to help people understand each other and the organization environment, thereby reducing anxiety and confusion. As solutions to internal and external problems are developed, they become shared assumptions. Over time, the assumptions may become so familiar that organizational members are no longer consciously aware of them.

Leader Influence on Culture

By changing or strengthening the culture of an organization, a manager influences the motivation and behavior of its members (Yukl).

Leaders can influence the culture of an organization in a variety of ways. According to Schein, there are five primary devices that offer the greatest potential for embedding and reinforcing culture:

- Attention. Managers communicate their priorities, values, and concerns by their choice of things to ask about and measure.
- Reactions to crises. A manager's response to a crisis can send a strong message about values and assumptions. A manager who faithfully supports espoused values during difficult times communicates the importance of the values.
- Role modeling. Managers communicate values by their own actions. A manager who walks the walk and talks the talk helps reinforce value importance.
- Allocation of rewards. The criteria used for allocating rewards signal what is valued by the organization. Formal recognition in ceremonies and informal praise communicate a manager's priorities.
- Selection and dismissal. Managers can influence organizational culture by their choice of criteria for recruiting, promoting, and firing people.

Culture and Organizational Stage

The influence of a leader on the culture of an organization varies depending on the developmental stage of the organization. For example, the founding manager of a new organization has a strong influence on imbedding its culture. This is due mainly to the founder's position of influence in molding new culture. However, creating culture may involve considerable conflict if the founding manager's ideas are not successful or if there are other powerful members of the organization with competing ideas. To succeed, the founder needs an appropriate vision and the ability and persistence to influence others to accept it (Kets de Vries & Miller).

The culture in young, successful organizations is likely to be strong because it is fundamental to the organization's success, the assumptions have been adopted by members, and the founding manager is still available for reinforcement of founding principles (Trice & Beyer). Eventually, as the organization matures and the founding manager moves on, the culture becomes less distinctive. Subcultures develop in different departments that may lead to conflicts and power struggles.

In general, it is more difficult to change the culture of an organization than to create culture in a new organization (Trice & Beyer). There are several reasons for this difficulty. Many of the underlying beliefs and assumptions shared by people in an organization are not consciously acknowledged. These cultural assumptions usually help explain the past and serve as fundamental tenets of the organization. In a mature, relatively prosperous organization, culture influences leaders more than leaders influence culture. Drastic changes are unlikely unless there is a major crisis (Yukl).

Maintenance of Culture

Trice and Beyer suggest that the literature on a leader's influence on culture emphasizes situations in which a manager either makes changes in culture or establishes a new organization with a different culture. The way in which managers maintain existing culture in an organization has been largely ignored (Yukl). Although less dramatic than cultural change, cultural maintenance is important for the continued effectiveness of an organization.

In a period of stability and prosperity, it is appropriate to strengthen the existing culture to keep it consistent with the strategy (Schlit & Locke). The culture of an organization naturally evolves over time, and without strong cultural leadership, it can change in undesirable ways. Key values in the culture may slowly erode if top management ignores them.

Trice and Beyer formulated a model comparing cultural change and maintenance management. For both types of cultural leadership, the manager creates an impression of competence, articulates ideology, communicates strong convictions, communicates high expectations and confidence in followers, serves as a role model, and otherwise motivates follower commitment to the organization's objectives and strategies. However, there are also some important differences between the two types of cultural leadership, whether maintenance or innovator.

Cultural maintenance leaders make only incremental changes in strategies, and they affirm existing values and traditions. In contrast, cultural innovators advocate new strategies and changes in culture. These managers may need to be more influential in convincing their reports and in dealing with their opponents.

Use of Symbols, Slogans, and Rituals

A change in organizational ideology usually requires modification of organization culture. One way to influence the culture is to change forms such as symbols, slogans, and rituals (Trice & Beyer).

Rituals, ceremonies, and rites of passage can be used to strengthen identification with the organization as well as to emphasize core values. Orientation programs can be used to socialize new employees. Training programs can be used to teach the ideology of the organization. However, one study by Ardichvili, Cardozo, & Gasparishvili found that entrepreneurs are using work design and performance management programs more often than training and development to change organizational culture. Other approaches to change include mentors who model and teach key values and special assignments to work areas of the organization where the new culture is strong (Fisher).

Distinguishing Organizational Culture From Societal Culture

Some researchers, such as Erez & Earley, suggest that organizational cultures are formed as a function of the societal culture present within them. However, Hofstede, suggests that the concepts of organizational and societal culture are different. Organizational culture is comprised of members who most likely exercised some influence in their decision to join the organization, and could also decide to leave it. On the other hand, members are born into their societal culture without choice.

Summary

Individual values as a person's established, enduring beliefs and preferences about what is worthwhile and desirable, will differ to some degree across managers (Rokeach). Behavior is the manner of acting in a given circumstance—what a person says and how he or she says it—as observed by both that person and others. Behavior is influenced by a person's values and their particular circumstances (Bales). Understanding that values tend to reflect important events and influences can be helpful in gaining insight into and predicting behavior. The argument was made (Merritt) that leader values influence behavior. And, that these independent variables influence employee organizational culture.

Values have become a central topic in the study of leadership. As you read in the first chapter, there have been a number of attempts to explain leadership in terms of models.

Several current studies focus on values as a central component of leadership. Others integrate values into a larger framework of variables that influences leadership. This chapter emphasizes the elements of meaning and direction as the key functions of leadership.

Meaning is a concept that conceptualizes the leader as the person who represents the value system of the group he or she is leading. Direction is a concept that represents group direction, such as where the group is headed. The Functional Approach is comprehensive in that it can help integrate several theories within its framework. It is not necessarily a unified theory. However, it is a theory that can accommodate other approaches to values.

One should attempt to read widely about the concept of values. Perception and philosophy are two areas of study that help explain how values play a part in shaping a group and how values guide one's actions and behavior.

As you read, try to imagine yourself in a present or past work situation and refer to that (or those) leadership environment(s). Close investigation should shed light on how values affect purpose and how purpose affects operations.

Approaches to Leadership

Some researchers have taken the view that the appropriate approach to understanding leadership is to study leaders' behaviors, traits and characteristics. However, over time this method has not revealed either the depth or breadth of significant data, as researchers had hoped. After considerable study, there are no consistent characteristics or behavior patterns, which define an effective leader.

A somewhat more convenient approach to understanding leaders was in analyzing the conditions and situations under which leadership takes place. While this approach to studying leadership showed promise, it also turned out to be less than acceptable, primarily because leadership takes place under a wide array of circumstances with an almost infinite number of micro conditions present in defining a discrete situation. Therefore, it is almost impossible, certainly impractical, to try to list every circumstance and condition that could define a situation.

There have also been attempts to correlate certain leadership characteristics with environmental characteristics in an attempt to help discover the most effective leadership style given specific environmental variables. However, as was the case with the conditions and situation approach, the variables that interact to determine an effective leadership style are enormous. It became an extremely difficult exercise to develop algorithms that could accurately determine relationships among traits, environmental characteristics, and effectiveness.

All of these approaches have been less than acceptable because they have not identified reliable elements that constitute a consistent leadership framework. In order for a leadership element to be considered reliable, it must satisfy one condition: the element produces factors that are consistent from one leadership situation to another. Even if consistent leadership elements are identified, it is obvious that no concept of leadership could be considered all-inclusive. The very nature of leadership is conceptual. We probably will never develop an algorithm for each situation that would guarantee leadership effectiveness.

One element that does seem to relate consistently to leadership is the values of a leader and those of his or her followers. The values of leaders and followers do affect leadership environments with reliability.

Values

Group values can seem abstract. However, values become operational and thereby identifiable through the vision, mission, goals, and objectives that are established by groups.

If group members adopt and conform to a set of values, it is almost certain that group members want and expect their leaders to conform to a similar set of values. The reality that rational followers perceive is the same reality that they want for their leaders to perceive, as well. It is reasonable to assume that if followers in a group setting are free to choose their leaders, they will choose and promote leaders who perpetuate the particular group's values. This is true whether the group is the American public electing a president, a school district electing a board member, or a quality assurance group at an automobile plant electing a team leader and spokesperson. Group members logically prefer a leader who represents most closely the group's value perceptions. The important message for the leader in this discussion is that leader values and his or her consequential behavior (the operationalization of values) must be perceived by the followers to mirror a value system of the followers, which becomes the culture of that group. The effective leader must support and otherwise champion goals and objectives that reflect the group's values in order to maintain long-term group support.

Meaning and Direction

As groups change in size and makeup, their values and goals evolve over time. As part of this natural evolution, polarizing elements will develop that challenge the group's original purpose and intent. Conflict and confrontation occur, which evidence one of the primary forces behind leadership: That the leadership environment is constantly changing. Effective leaders must remain cognizant of and responsive to such change in order to maintain their leadership status. They must effectively forecast and lead appropriate change. Hence the term, leader.

The effects of change may be as far reaching as to alter group values. The concept of meaning is introduced to help demonstrate how group values relate to leadership. Meaning in this context represents the essence of a group. It is the ethical foundation (as in group ethic), which makes the group what it is. It is important to note that the term ethical foundation in this context is not intended to include religious or moral overtones, unless the leader is leading a religious group. Instead, ethical foundation is used to represent the group's basic beliefs, such as group ethic.

On the surface, it appears that the most important leader action is to achieve the group's goals and objectives. However, real leadership action leads to realizing group meaning. Although the successful accomplishment of goals and objectives is important, it is the realization of the values that speak to the key purpose of leadership. Ideally, accomplishment of goals and objectives will yield realization of values but that is not necessarily correct.

For leader action to be of substance, the group's goals and objectives must reflect the group's values. Because of the vague nature of values, there is not always an obvious link between goals and values. The accomplishment of goals should be the tangible evidence of fulfilling values, if the two are significantly related. It is a group's values from which real group purpose is formulated, and it is values that provide the leader with substance for providing leadership. Thus, the first primary function of leadership resides in the concept of meaning. It is the leader's responsibility to communicate values that are important to the group, and this can only be done through action—his or her behavior. Action to realize group meaning implies direction. The second primary function of leadership is direction.

Direction as a concept is the course of action (behavior) that the leader uses to realize group meaning. Direction should relate directly to tasks, goals and objectives, and mission, just as meaning should be linked to group values. The saying applies: "If you do not know where you are going, then any path will work nicely." An effective leader must have a clear sense of direction in order to accomplish group goals. Without clear direction, goals will not be realized, the meaning of the group will not be realized.

A leader's effectiveness will be evaluated by group members' perception of the leader's support in realizing group values. The ideal leader should exemplify the values of the leader and follower environment, and provide acceptable direction to realize those values. Bernard Bass expresses the manner in which group values affect group members:

"Anyone born into a culture conforms to the same value orientation in order to be accepted and remain in the same social order. Deviation is likely to result in rejection and loss of esteem among the rest of the members sharing the cultural values."

Functional Approach

Although groups may require leaders to demonstrate certain skills and behaviors under certain conditions, not all behavior of a person in a leadership position can be accurately referred to as leadership behavior. Leadership's basic nature can be lost if skills, circumstances, and conditions are not taken into consideration as being a function of values.

Leader behavior, leadership environment, goals, objectives, etc. are symptomatic conditions of the essence of leadership. Using the functional model, all leader and follower behavior, conditions, and situations surrounding the leadership environment are accurately viewed within the context of how meaning and direction relate to group values. The major question becomes: How effectively does the leader portray group values, and will the direction that the leader prescribes move the group toward realization of its basic value system?

This does not imply that the study of leader behavior—analyzing the leadership environment, scrutinizing follower perceptions, and the like—is not important, because it is important. However, meaning and direction are the core elements that can be found in all effective leadership.

A leader's actions must include the following three dimensions or the actions should not be considered acts of leadership.

1. The group consists of rational people;
2. Specific group ethical and directional elements (which may change over time) can be identified, and
3. A leader or leaders can be identified within the group.

If values vary from group to group and situation to situation, then values are relative. A group's ethical (as in group ethic) foundation (value structure) affects the group's collective perception of reality. The cause and effect interactions between values and environmental factors affect perception of reality and determine the mix of variables that the group uses as criteria for group membership. Therefore, for any particular group, reality is a function of value perceptions. Hence, a group's collective view of reality is the ultimate criterion for choosing, following, and evaluating who is to lead and who will be members of the group.

The functional approach is rooted in the group's beliefs, values, and principles—the group's ethical foundation. The concept of meaning may be thought of as the leader being the role model who characteristically reflects the principles, values, beliefs, and dogmas. The concept of direction may be thought of as the course a leader plots to achieve and or realize group meaning. Direction is not so much the act of directing people as it is the overall course of action that moves the group toward realizing its essence. The primary functions of a leader are to exemplify group values, and to communicate meaning to the group so that the group has a clear understanding of group purpose, intent, and direction.

The functional approach gives purpose to the leader's action and behavior, and provides substance for the group's mission.

Leadership Propositions

There are several assumptions that concluded from the study of theories and concepts that affect leadership. These statements take the form of propositions that encourage further inquiry.

1. Leadership is universal. Leadership occurs in every situation where people come together with common goals and missions.

2. Leadership usually takes place in a group setting. Leadership is typically defined in terms of some group function.

3. Leadership is not a position or a set of characteristics that exists within an organizational structure. Positions do not lead others, people lead others. Leadership characteristics are only exhibited by people. One may have expectations of leadership from people in positions that require leadership, but a position (per se) cannot lead.

4. Two skills are essential for effective leadership: Motivation and assessment. The leader must get followers to act (motivation) toward group goals and the leader must be able to recognize (assessment) when the goals are being reached. Motivation and assessment skills may also be supported by other skills of varying degrees. However, whatever other skills are necessary, the end-result is that they must be used effectively to motivate the group and assess the group's progress toward its goals.

5. The skills necessary to be an effective leader depend upon the circumstances and conditions under which the leader is acting. The type of skills may depend on group size and purpose, and where the leader fits into the group's formal structure (This is particularly true in today's corporate structures).

6. The primary leadership functions include meaning and direction. This is a functional approach to defining the nature of leadership.

7. Leaders should exemplify the ethical foundation of the group. The leader should unify group goals, values, principles, beliefs, and dogmas and provide a direction of action so that these goals can be realized.

8. Leadership is situational. A leader may be successful in some situations and unsuccessful in others.
9. More than one leader may emerge from within a group. Leadership is not confined to one person.
10. A follower's readiness and skill level determine the effective style for a leader to adopt.
11. Certain leadership styles in particular situations are desirable over other styles. The adoption of an effective leadership style is dependent on the particular situation in the leadership environment.
12. A leader's actions have an effect on group attitude. A leader's actions influence general interactions of group members as they work toward realizing the group's purpose and intent.
13. In many cases, it takes time for a leader's actions to manifest into group conscience. It also takes time for the leader's actions to have bearing on results.
14. A leader's general attitude toward people will affect how the particular leader relates to people. Attitudes permeate one's actions whether they are leaders or followers.
15. Organizational structure and a group's managerial philosophies affect a leader's preferred leadership style. The group climate affects leadership style.
16. Leaders can be successful without being effective. To be effective, followers must have positive feelings about success.
17. Leaders' actions that are not group-goal-directed cannot be referred to as leader actions.
18. The nature of the contact (such as, daily, weekly, formal, informal) that the leader has with followers will determine, to a large extent, the leadership style that is most effective for that group.

The purpose of presenting these preceding propositions is to initiate discussion and thought concerning leadership. Exploring some of the propositions may lead to new thinking about leadership, and may one day provide the information for a more detailed and scientific investigation of the subject.

There are also terms and suppositions that could be considered by-products of these propositions:

1. Accessibility to a leader by the followers affects the followers' perceptions of leader behavior. The more direct access a follower has to the leader; the better a follower is able to assess the leader's behavior.
2. Leadership is a function of meaning and direction. Leadership's primary function is to provide a group with a consolidated view of the group's values and provide direction to realize these values.
3. Group diversity increases difficulty in consolidating group meaning. This seems reasonable since there would be various values, principles and beliefs to encounter.
4. Group size affects a leader's role in providing group direction.
5. As groups increase in size, administrative and managerial functions necessary to accomplish group goals, increase.
6. Complexity of a group's vision, mission, goals, and objectives has bearing on the functions of meaning and direction.

Although it is not possible to develop a neat formula for successful leadership, it is important to know as much about the elements that affect leadership as possible. If elements can be identified and put together in such a manner that it helps explain leadership conditions and interacting forces, it will help the student of leadership to understand the nature of effective leadership.

General Review

Leaders exist to help fulfill the purpose and intent of the groups that they lead. This may seem to be an elementary statement, but the implications are far-reaching.

- Group purpose and intent is a reflection of why a group exists, and is more deeply a statement directly related to ethic—the group's bonding element. This bonding element will be termed the ethical foundation of a group.
- The ethical foundation is the cornerstone of group values;
- A group's values become the foundation for the philosophy of the group;

- Philosophy will dictate the group purpose; and
- Purpose is directly accessible through group policies, objectives and goals.

Thus, one may determine a group's ethical foundation by analyzing its policies, goals and objectives. Admittedly, other sources of information would need to be included in order to gain an understanding of a group's values, but goals, objectives, and policies seem to be a logical starting place.

Leadership is universal; it takes place within all group settings. Group, in this context, is a collection of people who are brought together for common goals and purposes and bound by certain philosophical ideas, beliefs, and moral persuasions. Therefore, a group could be a nation, club, school, society, marriage, or any other situation in which two or more people bind themselves for specific purposes. Using this line of reasoning, purpose relates directly to the group's ethical foundation; thus, the core of leadership revolves around values.

A group's ethical foundation affects the perception of leader performance. It is apparent that groups operate and develop expectations of their leaders based on the group's particular beliefs, values, and principles. Since group ethical foundations may vary from group to group, groups will develop particular leader expectations. And, these groups will develop their own unique criteria for evaluating their leadership.

It is clear that expectations are linked to beliefs. Beliefs, in this sense, relate to the ambiance of group beliefs and are a reflection of the group's ethical system. It is also clear that people group themselves according to their beliefs and values.

Environmental factors, such as catastrophes, economic conditions, political conditions, and the like will affect the leadership style preferred by and appropriate for a group. Unexpected and or other major events occur, which affect a group's value structure. When this occurs, the values of the group will shift, quite possibly affecting the group's perception of the leadership role.

Chapter 04:

The Leadership Environment

Introduction

This chapter revisits the term leader and presents questions about the leader. You no doubt have developed ideas about leadership from past experience and the text. So, these questions should encourage you to think critically about elements that go into helping mold and shape leaders in their organizational environments.

Environment is a term used conceptually to represent the ambient surroundings—the workplace—of the leader and follower. What are some of the symbols we use to communicate more effectively? Why are they important? What part does our society play in shaping our ideas about how things should be? Is it important for us to know about symbols in our environments and society at large in studying leadership? Does the way in which we communicate effect how others perceive us? All of these questions are obviously important to the leader and the leadership environment. However, an even more overriding question for a student of leadership might be to ask, how do we frame these and other important topics in order to develop a coherent field of study?

This chapter attempts to present some of these concepts with the hope of bringing closure to the text. Knitting these concepts together is a difficult task. You should be at a point in your study that you should be able to analyze this chapter and understand the importance of each topic both as it relates to other concepts and to the larger concept of leadership itself. Your readings and writings on the topic of leadership should enable you to initiate and synthesize thought on the topic, and formulate original ideas for response during discussion.

Background

The theories that have been discussed in the preceding chapters involve three foci:

1. The leader
2. The followers or
3. The environment

Almost anything that can be written about leadership involves one or some combination of these three areas. Gaining knowledge of leadership preferences and styles, identifying wants and needs of followers, and becoming familiar with the organizational environment becomes a fundamental analysis to anyone who finds him or herself in a leadership situation. Upon reviewing the definition of leadership, it is obvious that these three areas are conceptually related. The definition restated:

Leadership is the action of inducing and or influencing followers to accomplish certain goals that represent the values, wants and needs, aspirations and expectations of both leader and follower.

While reference to both leader and follower appear in this definition, the leadership environment is clearly implied.

By stating that it is necessary to understand group goals, we emphasize that effective leaders and followers must understand where the group is heading. One prerequisite for reaching a goal is effective communication. In order for the group to move toward common objectives, an understanding of the leadership environment must encompass the values of the leader and followers, and those of the general environment. The leader must understand and adapt to the style in order to be effective. The followers must perceive the leader as a person who represents group values, and the followers must also perceive the direction being proposed as one that will effectively achieve group goals.

That is not to say that persons who gain knowledge about their leadership environment will become successful leaders. The essence of this proposition is that knowledge in these three areas is a prerequisite for a successful and efficient group and leader situation.

The question then becomes one of how do we choose an appropriate leadership style, and how do we recognize when we are becoming effective leaders. For many, this knowledge is gained through experience—trial and error. People learn about life by living. As indicated earlier, there is no specific formula for understanding leadership. Therefore, one may have to experience leadership situations one at a time to enable him or her to establish and categorize general propositions about leadership. Ideally, these categories are filed away in a leader's memory to be called upon when a similar situation occurs; whereupon the leader considers and then either 1) acts or 2) adds new information, modifies the category, and then acts.

The Leader

Are you a leader? What type leader are you? What are some of the characteristics that help make a person capable of being a leader? Is leadership training necessary? What personal attributes must a leader possess? What skills must a leader know? These are questions that many people want to answer when they take a leadership course.

By studying theories in Chapter 01, we discovered that we might label leaders by their behavior, personality, and or situational circumstances. Some theories promote a leader as being born with certain characteristics that allow him or her to assume roles of leadership. Other theories promote education and training as the necessary ingredient for obtaining leadership qualities. Leaders' actions have been used to identify style and terms have been adopted to describe the relationships between leaders and followers.

The terms directing, coaching, supporting, delegating, and others were used to describe the leader. Other theories attempted to describe the leader in terms of their character traits. For example, the leader is intelligent, brave, fair-minded, loyal, trustworthy, friendly, true, etc. Through the course of studying leadership, it should have become evident that there are neither behavior styles nor established traits that can automatically make a leader effective. Effective leadership depends on style, traits, environmental conditions, maturity of the group, and other variables in specific circumstances.

Some leadership courses administer personality tests to identify personality traits of the subjects. The purpose for this is to identify individuals' behavioral preferences when dealing with people and situations. There is some usefulness to this approach, but one should not rely on this type of analysis as providing necessarily reliable data. Personality tests of this type provide generalized descriptions and may not consider changes in behavior that occur after training or education. Personality is an important area to investigate in learning more about how a person may view followers and the leadership situation.

Theory X and Y attempt to categorize how people view one another. By identifying how a person views others, an attempt is made to reveal how that person may react to others. This theory provides one way of predicting how one may generally behave or react in the face of certain events.

Evidence gained from the results of personality tests and knowing one's general attitudes toward others may be helpful in understanding actions taken in the leadership environment. If we know why people may behave as they do, we may be able to change behavior that does not produce desirable results. If people can be taught to change behaviors, then they may be taught to be leaders. This is a key assumption behind the question: Are leaders born or can one be trained to lead? A similar question that seeks leadership information: Is leadership more an art or a science? The answers to these questions are not conclusive. Many leadership researchers would suggest these observations:

- Leadership is part art and part science, suggesting that it is both an art and a science.
- Some may be born with or grow up influenced by external variables (taught) which foster tendencies toward and an interest in and leadership.
- It is reasonable to assume that education and training may be the tools through which one learns or enhances leadership behavior.

It is not easy to determine which components interact in varying proportions to yield an effective leader.

It would be helpful for the prospective leader to gain insight into how he or she may be perceived by others. Knowing one's self and knowing how others perceive us is one of the first rules for becoming an effective leader. However, this is no easy task. At times, it is difficult to know our true selves because we fail to do (or may be incapable of doing) honest self-appraisals. Similarly, it is no easy task to know how others perceive us because we may not really want to know or others may be afraid to tell us.

We may gain information on how others perceive us in several manners.

- Ask others. The leader may solicit information from individual followers concerning their perception of the leader. This approach may have several drawbacks, the obvious one being that a follower may be unwilling to provide a true assessment to someone who may have an influence over rewarding or punishing them.

- Survey others. An indirect approach to gain the same information may also be taken. One way is by conducting a survey, asking followers how they would evaluate areas for which the leader has control. Areas such as morale, communications, productivity, and the like are within the purview of most leaders. These general areas are probably good assessment points to obtain a picture of how the leader is viewed by followers.

Note that if followers are negative about much of the work environment, such as poor facilities, unsafe working conditions, and negative human resource policies, it is unlikely the leader will be perceived as being highly effective. One drawback to surveying is that followers may not have a complete picture of the leader and may not understand the global view that affects the leadership environment.

In knowing one's self, it may be helpful for leaders to know their predominate personality traits. It may be surprising to realize that followers do not rate leaders the same that leaders would rate themselves. It is convenient to overestimate one's abilities and effectiveness when self-interests are involved.

Thus, self-evaluations often fall to personal bias and thereby do not produce accurate assessments.

Evaluating leader behavior, personality, and ability will probably be somewhat biased, depending on the source of information. But, it is important for a leader to know how he or she is viewed and it is important to possess an accurate assessment of his or her abilities.

A personality test, a survey of follower opinions, a self-evaluation, and an assessment of the leader effectiveness would provide data useful in understanding the effectiveness of a leader. Overall, perhaps none is more accurate than another is, as they all have their strengths and drawbacks. Therefore, effective leaders are wise to use a combination of methods. Leaders must maintain a constant assessment of the perceptions of followers in order to determine the most effective leadership style to adopt.

Knowing One's Self

Over time, theorists, researchers, and effective leaders have stressed the importance of leaders understanding themselves more thoroughly before they can become effective leaders of others. We introduced the concept of situational leadership (Hersey & Blanchard) earlier in the text. We have also discussed several types of behavioral tests and surveys designed to assist leaders in learning more about themselves. We will present several diagnostic tools in the form of exercises to assist you in learning more about yourself as a leader. As you complete these exercises, it is helpful to reflect on how they affect who you are as a leader. Note that these exercises may be available as assignments, handouts, and or worksheets.

Environment

The leadership environment encompasses all variables external to the leader that affect leader efficiency and success. In order to examine the leadership environment it is necessary to examine how people interact within this environment.

Symbols. Knowing how people interact is very important, especially when cooperation among people is necessary. One method of communication is by using symbols. Symbols are usually subtle and it takes understanding the undertones of an environment to realize their full meaning.

Warren Bennis, one of the major researchers of leadership over the past many years states that the extent to which leadership is truly effective is based on the extent to which individuals place symbolic value on leader intentions. Most environments are loaded with symbolism. Their use helps communicate real and deep feelings that people have about values and issues. Picture for a moment some of the major symbols used throughout the world: A corner office with a view, the American Flag (or any other country's flag), the skull and crossbones on a pirate ship, a gold star in class, etc. Symbols are usually subtle (picture a successful businessperson wearing an Armani suit), while others are blatantly obvious (picture a hate group burning a cross in someone's front yard). Whether subtle or obvious, people communicate with symbols. Symbols represent a way for people to communicate and or otherwise help reinforce their beliefs, values, and traditions. Effective leaders should understand how their followers interpret and value symbols. Some symbols come and go in a culture, while others are more long lasting. Whatever their duration, symbols communicate meaning. How we use and view symbols is important in interpretation of the reality they represent. Earlier in the text, we covered the concept of perception. Symbols, most certainly, play an important role in forming and supporting the perceptions of both leaders and followers. Effective leaders look for the undertones in symbols in order to understand their broader meaning.

Society. Society, as a whole, plays a major role in the formation of groups as well as their interaction. Thus, society plays an important role in the concept of leadership. Within this context, society represents the big picture values, principles, and mores that are accepted and practiced by the mainstream of people within a particular culture.

The Encarta dictionary defines society in terms of relationships among groups as the sum of social relationships among groups of humans or animals. Similarly, it defines society in terms of a structured community of people as a community bound together by similar traditions, institutions, or nationality.

One often-used cultural comparison is between the United States and Japan. This interest is perhaps due to the economic competition between the two countries. I will use these two countries as examples of how different cultures view elements that influence leadership.

Many articles have been written about how leadership styles are affected by cultural characteristics. Several studies have compared and contrasted cultures, and found that the differences have a major influence on preferred leadership styles. One study (Bass and Burgher) discovered a cultural propensity in the U.S. toward entrepreneurship and resourcefulness. Japanese people, on the other hand, seem to prefer to use intuition. The Japanese think in long-term perspectives while the U.S. is culturally geared toward shorter-term perspectives.

Communication. As the world becomes an instantaneous communication system, the societies of the world have become more accessible and available. As a result, information moves very quickly among localities, states, nations, and continents. What happens in Russia one morning can affect western economic markets, such as those of the U.S., before noon. Effective leaders must be aware of the impact—both positive and negative—of swift communication. Leaders must consider public opinion and its consequential effect on organizations, groups, and institutions. Warren Bennis notes the importance of leaders in effectively managing public relations. Leaders, in their decision-making roles, are becoming increasingly involved in the managing of external constituencies in order to provide thoroughness of leadership.

Cultures are becoming entwined and intermingled and there seems to be no set of rules in dealing with cultural interaction. At times, it appears that the strong survive or at least the strongest hand rules the day. Leadership, whether it is within a group that has minor involvement or whether it is leading a multinational corporation, is affected by the availability of instantaneous communication. Communication has become a power that influences leadership.

Followers

Groups. The term followers is used contextually in the text to describe a group or team. Studying group behavior and group characteristics are important conceptual components of leadership. Leadership involves actions taken by a person, which are centered on a particular group. A group comes together for specific reasons in a manner that their collective actions assist in accomplishing group goals. Since groups are goal directed, a major function of the leader is to accomplish group goals in the most effective way possible. Therefore, to be effective the leader one must have an understanding of the people in the group, their reasons for being group members, and group dynamics in the way that they interact.

If group goals are simple, there may be little emphasis placed on planning and development. If group goals are complex and the organization is complex, planning and development may be key factors in the structure of the organization. If group goals are complex, then communication may become a critical element to the success of the entire organization. Group interaction and the complexity for each set of circumstances must be identified in order to understand the dynamics of any particular group. Understanding these dynamics is not as simple as learning how to conduct a successful meeting. Understanding group dynamics means knowing why and how people within groups interact. This is a far more complicated scenario than following rules for group meetings.

At times people become confused when the subject of group dynamics is addressed. They tend to think of group meetings and the things that go on in meetings. This may be an element of group dynamics, but the term implies much more. A group may be defined as the entire body of people who work for an organization or it may be a small work group that consists of just two people. The group dynamics include all of the interactions that take place, whether in meetings or between or among individuals. Several variables influence groups:

- Size
- Complexity

- Task
- Relations
- Working conditions.

An understanding of motivational theories and organizational behavior are two areas of study that are necessary components for leaders of large organizations.

There are some helpful hints about meeting dynamics that leaders need to know. Research has found that groups are usually more willing to take risk (than individuals), and that if the group leader does not commit to a specific course of action, the group will develop alternative courses of action with greater creativity. Group unity and morale is of constant concern to the leader. All groups must feel single minded in their purpose in order to realize true success. To understand how groups function, there have been several codification systems developed.

Classifying Groups. Robert Owens developed a classification system to help describe group characteristics. He conceived that an effective group could be defined and differentiated by at least three characteristics:

- Members of a group are interdependent: they share with others certain values, beliefs, attitudes, knowledge and fears. This interdependence is expressed through interaction between and among members of the group, such as by communicating, sharing and engaging in rituals.
- Members of a group derive satisfaction of individual needs from being part of the group. These needs include issues such as safety, security, belonging, and esteem. The satisfaction of these needs is not readily observable in the behavior of individuals but must be inferred from their patterns of behavior.
- Members of a group share goals. A group seeks to achieve specific objectives or goals. To achieve these goals, the members of the group must interact and must derive satisfaction from the interaction processes, as well as from goal achievement itself.

There are several important implications in the above listed three characteristics. Satisfying individual needs as well as group goals is the balancing act that makes or breaks the group. If an individual's needs are not being met by group membership, it is likely the person will not remain a group member. If group goals are not being met, it is likely the group will falter. Therefore, harmony must exist between satisfying individual needs and accomplishing group goals.

One example of individual needs and group goal conflict can be illustrated by examining the labor union movement in America. Unions have traditionally represented concerns of employees, while management has represented company interests. In many cases, these two factions have been in conflict over employee concerns and company concerns. To survive, companies must be competitive in their respective markets. On the other hand, in order for families to survive, employees must earn adequate salaries and benefits. It is clear that needs exist for both individuals and the company. World economies are in a state of flux and it is evident in the U.S. that many organizations are having trouble. Some companies have not survived. Unions have lost strength as organizations are cutting back on permanent work forces and outsourcing in many areas.

The point of this example is to illustrate that groups exist side-by-side with conflicting interests. This is an example of how group dynamics are affected by variables of conflicting interest. Groups may have common goals but there may be internal conflict about how things will operate. This illustration does not typify all groups. One could examine another type of group where conflict of this nature does not exist. One thing is certain, groups differ in their wants and needs.

Group Climate. Successful groups may be identified by how they accomplish goals. Leaders of effective groups seem to stand out in the crowd. In a survey of followers over a two-year period, specific adjectives were commonly used to identify the effective leader. These terms have been used to describe the effective leader and the climate in which effective leadership takes place. The most common of these terms are listed below.

The terms themselves are not surprising. However, the interpretation of these terms varies greatly

Leader
- Strong
- Warm
- Friendly
- Smart
- Helpful
- Fair
- Supportive
- Confident
- Effective Communicator
- Admired

Group
- Proud
- Efficient
- Successful
- Elite
- Unique
- Friends
- Positive Attitude
- Dependable

Climate
- Enjoyable
- Rewarding
- Good Morale
- Success Oriented
- Competitive
- Friendly
- Responsibility
- Clear Direction
- Goals Identified
- Rewards Identified

These terms may aid in explaining how people feel about a successful and effective group setting. Others respond with similar language, which can roughly be classified under the aforementioned terms into the three areas. The overarching message to leaders is that they should strive to create a positive group climate, forge interpersonal relationships, and develop skills that group members perceive as being success oriented. These terms help formulate perceptions of group members that produce group reality.

Follower perception of leader action is the driving force behind group success. How a particular leader acts may not have as much impact on the group as a follower's perception of those actions. Thomas Sergiovanni points out that real meaning in leadership rests with the meanings, which become more important than the actions themselves. He emphasizes the long-term by stating that leaders must move beyond the obvious and focus on the subtleties of long-term effort to bring about effective leadership. The real value of leadership rests with the effects of actions on others rather than the actions themselves. The implication is that the perception a follower derives from a leader's action is the essence of leadership behavior.

If a leader intends one thing by certain actions but followers perceive another, then the leader's action does not serve the leader's intended purpose. The perception a group gets from a leader's behavior has more bearing on the ultimate fate of the group than what the leader perceives. Many times we see the clarity of situations and wonder why others do not or cannot see it the same way. However, some of the most severe difficulties between leaders and followers come from simple miscommunication and misperception of one sort or another. It is apparent that leaders must consistently be mindful as to how their actions are being perceived by others.

Article 01:

The Effect of Leader Values on Behavior

Article authors: Edward A. Merritt and Dennis Reynolds

Abstract

The purpose of this study was to examine the interpersonal work values of leaders in work settings and to determine the influence of such variables on their consequential behavior. A total of 301 participant managers were drawn from private industry. A survey questionnaire, personal interviews, and unobtrusive observation methods were utilized. Checks were used to verify that the data were free from regional and organizational bias, test for response stability, and guard against response bias. Support was found for the hypothesis that manager values and certain demographic variables of interest will lead to manager behavior. Applications, limitations, and research implications are discussed.

Introduction

Values are attitudes about what is correct and incorrect, fair and unfair, honorable and dishonorable (Yukl, 1998). Examples include fairness, integrity, trustworthiness, courtesy, and support. Values are salient because they influence manager choices, awareness, and behavior, which, in turn influence and shape the work place. Manager values and their consequential behavior play an important part in shaping organizations. In this research, work values held by leaders were investigated.

A second concept that is addressed is that of managerial behavior. The concept of managerial behavior suggests that managers may use certain behavior in order to contend with the varying demands of their positions.

There is a gap in the research that addresses work values and behavior of managers, the subject of this study.

Background

Values are fundamental convictions that a certain mode of behavior or end result state is preferable to a converse mode or end result existence (Rokeach, 1973). Values have nested within them an element of judgment in that they are a reflection of an individual's or group's belief about what is right, desirable, or good. Values have attributes regarding content and attributes that regulate intensity. The content attribute states that some behavior or end result is desirable. The intensity attribute states the importance of such behavior or end state. By ranking values by intensity, an idea of a person's individual or work group's value system can be obtained (Bales, 1999; Bales & Cohen, 1979).

Values are important to the study of management and organizational culture because they help establish a foundation for the understanding of attitudes and motivation and because they influence perceptions, attitudes, and behavior (Connor & Becker, 1994). Individuals enter organizations with interpretations and ideas of what should and should not be. Furthermore, such interpretations imply that some behavior or end states are preferable to others. As a result, individuals' value systems may be incongruent with those of the organization. With an increasing demand by consumers for a higher level and quality of service (Cline, 1996; Coyle & Dale, 1993; Zeithaml, Parasuraman, & Berry, 1990), the effect of values on employee organizational culture becomes a key issue to help ensure that individual value systems are aligned with those of the employing organization's staff, in order to meet such demand.

Individual values as a person's established, enduring beliefs and preferences about what is worthwhile and desirable will differ to some degree across managers (Rokeach, 1973). Behavior is the manner of acting in a given circumstance--what a person says and how he or she says it--as observed by that person and others. Behavior is influenced by a person's values and his or her particular circumstances (Bales, 1970). Understanding that values tend to reflect important events and influences can be helpful in gaining insight into and predicting behavior.

This study, then, is designed to determine the work values of leaders and to study the relationship of this variable to the outcome variable of manager behavior.

Literature Review

In 1956, Bronowski stated that values are deep interpersonal illuminations of justice and injustice, good and bad, and means and ends. Expanding this, Rokeach (1973) defined values as abiding ideology that one mode of conduct or end state is preferable to another mode of conduct or end state. Hofstede (1991) interpreted this definition more holistically and suggested that values are manifestations of one's basic approach toward life—broad tendencies to favor specific states over others—to which Schwartz (1996) added that values equate to transsituational goals that vary in importance, and serve as guiding principles. Yukl (1998) expanded this further and defined values as attitudes about what is right and wrong, ethical and unethical, moral and immoral; examples include fairness, honesty, loyalty, courtesy, and cooperation. Coalescing the preceding definitions,

Bales (1999) defined values as enduring, trait-like, and high-order abstractions in the mind of a person, which correlate fantasies, images, perceptions, and concepts. Central to the study reported here, then, this definition suggests that values are an individual's lens through which he or she interprets experiences and their meanings. Moreover, this understanding of values underscores the construct's centrality to the self concept and suggests values influence predominately behavior whether or not the individual thinks about values (Bales, 1999; Feather, 1992).

The literature review substantiates Bales' work in integrating interpersonal behavior and values. Many researchers treat behavior as phenomena characteristic of developing lists of traits. Others, such as McDougall (1918), and Lewin (1951), theorized that behavior is part of a higher-order system. In this higher-order system, values are considered to be more complex than behavior and the product of multiple filters.

For example, McClelland (1980) attested that values guide interpersonal behavior, and stated that they are best obtained from questionnaires and non-obtrusive observational methods. Triandis (1989) posited that values are a critical determinant of social behavior while Elizur et al. (1991) asserted that values motivate goal-directed behavior. More pointedly, Hofstede (1980, 1991) suggested that values determine the meanings of people's behavior.

Kluckhohn and Strodtbeck (1961) offer, from an anthropological perspective, their definition of value orientations as being complex, rank-ordered principles developing from cognitive, affective, and directive elements. And, such influences provide order and direction for the ever-changing situations. Feather (1992) contends that individual values, as they relate to behavior and social interaction, were largely ignored by psychologists in favor of behaviorism, personality theories, and group dynamics.

Bales (1999) suggested that behavior is observed. And, that once observed, certain evaluations are placed on such behavior. The evaluations inform a behavioral response to the original initiated act. These evaluations can be treated as sets of values held by both the observer and the person being observed. This builds on Bales' (1985) earlier contentions that values' primary focus is the evaluation tool for the behavior of the self and others in interaction. Thus, values and behavior are closely intertwined. Empirical evidence as to what moderates such a relationship, however, is lacking.

Methodology

This study utilized an integrated field theory of social psychology developed by Bales (Bales & Cohen, 1979) as a theoretical foundation and as a measurement system to investigate managerial work values and behavior. Field theory can be defined as a broad set of theories that focus on the total psychological environment and attempt to explain behavior because of interactions between people (Reber, 1995). The isomorphic properties of Bales' model make it possible to assess values and behavior using the same three-dimensional, factor-analytic framework (Bales, 1985, 1988; Bales & Cohen, 1979).

Using the values and behavior scale forms, participant managers' direct reports (such as department heads) considered the actual values and behavior of their managing supervisor when answering statements. The results of respondent statements were then examined in order to understand how these values related to the outcome variable of behavior.

The three bipolar dimensions for both the values and behavior scales are classified by using names that relate to their location in the model that resembles a three-dimensional schema:

- The Upward-Downward (U-D) dimension.
- The Positive-Negative (P-N) dimension.
- The Forward-Backward (F-B) dimension.

The three dimensions are measured independently of each other. For example, the U-D dimension is not affected by ratings on P-N or F-B. On the other hand, each of the dimensions is bipolar. For example, if a value or behavior measures as more of a dimension, such as "up" on the U-D dimension, that score, because of its bipolar nature, indicates a lack of "down" (Bachman, 1988; Hogan, 1988; Koenigs & Cowen, 1988). Therefore, the model measures the two ends of each of the three bipolar dimensions as well as the intermediate points between the ends.

First, the direct reports rated current work values. Second, the direct reports rated on-the-job behavior. The two questionnaires elicit responses about perceptions of the current interpersonal work values and behavior of their supervising managers.

Importance of the Study

This study has theoretical importance in that it will help provide a better understanding of managerial work-related values and behavior in the club industry. In this context, we contend that values help mold and direct the workplace behavior. Offering practical importance, This study explores whether the identification of groups of meanings expressed through values produce elements that may help in understanding an organization's behavior.

These groups of meanings are the foundations of behavior expressed as values and principles reflected in customs, traditions, and symbols. The central meanings are not discrete points. Instead, they represent ranges, which are recognized within an organization. In other words, values and behavior reflect a unique organization-wide variation in culture, which is as defined and as basic as is the variation in biological phenomena (Kluckhohn & Strodtbeck, 1961).

Previous research suggests that a blending of the positive components from the three dimensions of values and behavior in the workplace typically correlate with effective managerial outcomes (Bales & Isenberg, 1980; Hogan, 1988; Koenigs & Cowen, 1988). The question of interest involved investigating whether managerial values may predict behavior.

Findings

The research question: Do manager values and certain demographic variables of interest predict U-D, P-N, and F-B manager behavior?

Support was found for the hypothesis that manager values and certain demographic variables of interest will predict manager behavior.

Behavior U-D

Table1: Behavior U-D Model Summary

Model	R	R Square	Adjusted R Square	Std. Error of the Estimate
1	.573[a]	.328	.319	2.7433

a. Predictors: (Constant), Bonus Pay, Interaction Term
V_UD*V_PN, Values PN, Values UD

Predictors: (Constant), Bonus Pay, Interaction Term

Table 2: Behavior U-D ANOVA

Model		Sum of Squares	df	Mean Square	F	Sig.
1	Regression	1088.849	4	272.212	36.172	.000 [a]
	Residual	2227.575	296	7.526		
	Total	3316.424	300			

a. Predictors: (Constant), Bonus Pay, Interaction Term V_UD*V_PN, Values PN, Values UD

Table 3: Behavior U-D Coefficients

Model		Unstandardized Coefficients		Standardized Coefficients		
		B	Std. Error	Beta	t	Sig.
1	(Constant)	2.235	.448		4.990	.000
	Values UD	.961	.102	.682	9.445	.000
	Values PN	-4.376E-02	.062	-.049	-.706	.481
	Interaction Term V_UD*V_PN	-6.953E-02	.019	-.314	-3.585	.000
	Bonus Pay	.244	.097	.121	2.520	.012

The U-D (Up-Down) dimension of behavior scores can be predicted by the U-D dimension of values. This suggests that manager scores on the U dimensional element defined as "values on dominance" values or the D dimensional element defined as "values on submissiveness" values will reflect a positive relationship with the U dimensional element defined as "dominant" behavior or the D dimensional element defined as "submissive" behavior. Moreover, managers who have value sets that are more dominant--demonstrating value sets focusing on individual financial success, personal prominence, and power-- will likely display more dominant behavior. Managers who have value sets that are more submissive--demonstrating value sets focusing on giving up personal needs and desires, passivity-- will likely display more submissive behavior.

The U-D dimension of behavior scores can be predicted by the interaction of the U-D dimension of values and the P-N (Positive-Negative) dimension of values. This suggests that at any particular values U-D level, there is an inverse relationship between the interaction with values P-N in predicting the U-D dimension of behavior. Moreover, in the interaction, as the U dimensional element defined as "values on dominance" values element increases in values U-D, the P dimensional element defined as "values on friendly behavior" values in values P-N decreases. An inverse relationship is indicated between the interaction term and the U-D dimension of behaviors. This suggests that the interaction of managers who have more dominant values and who are also less friendly will exhibit more submissive behaviors.

The implications for application suggest that senior managers and boards of governors should carefully examine their hiring practices. If, for example, a more dominant manager is identified who is also less friendly, the corresponding behavior will likely be more submissive. On the other hand, if a more submissive manager is identified who is also friendlier, the finding suggests that the manager's behavior will be more dominant.

The U-D (Up-Down) dimension of behavior scores can be predicted by annualized bonus pay average. This suggests that managers who make more in bonus (the scale was an ordinal, continuous scale, which was used to rank-order level of bonus from less to more, including, 1."no bonus" to 7."30 percent or more of base") are also more dominant. Moreover, managers who make less in bonus are also more submissive.

The implications for application suggest that senior managers and boards of governors should carefully examine their bonus programs. If a more dominant manager is desirable for the club, consider increasing the bonus plan to the upper end of the scale toward 30 percent or more of base. If a less dominant (more submissive) manager is desirable, consider decreasing the bonus plan to the lower end of the scale toward zero.

Behavior P-N

Table 4: Behavior P-N Model Summary

Model	R	R Square	Adjusted R Square	Std. Error of the Estimate
1	.763[a]	.582	.578	2.9129

a. Predictors: (Constant), Married Yes or No, Values FB, Values PN

Table 5: Behavior P-N ANOVA

Model		Sum of Squares	df	Mean Square	F	Sig.
1	Regression	3508.349	3	1169.450	137.827	.000 [a]
	Residual	2520.017	297	8.485		
	Total	6028.365	300			

a. Predictors: (Constant), Married Yes or No, Values FB, Values PN

Table 6: Behavior P-N Coefficients

Model		Unstandardized Coefficients		Standardized Coefficients		
		B	Std. Error	Beta	t	Sig.
1	(Constant)	1.739	.543		3.203	.002
	Values PN	.807	.047	.673	17.168	.000
	Values FB	.233	.049	.183	4.723	.000
	Married Yes or No	1.441	.491	.112	2.936	.004

The P-N (Positive-Negative) dimension of behavior scores can be predicted by the P-N dimension of values. This suggests that manager scores on the P dimensional element defined as "values on friendly behavior" or the N dimensional element defined as "values on unfriendly behavior" will reflect a positive relationship with the P dimensional element defined as "friendly" behavior or the N dimensional element defined as "unfriendly" behavior. Moreover, managers who are more friendly-- demonstrating value sets focusing on equality and democratic participation in decision making--will likely display more friendly behavior. Managers who are more unfriendly--demonstrating value sets focusing on self-protection, self-interest first, and self-sufficiency--will likely display more unfriendly behavior.

The P-N (Positive-Negative) dimension of behavior scores can be predicted by the F-B (Forward-Backward) dimension of values. This suggests that manager scores on the F dimensional element defined as "values on accepting task orientation of established authority" or the B dimensional element defined as "values on opposing task orientation of established authority" will reflect a positive relationship with the P dimensional element defined as "friendly" behavior or the N dimensional element defined as "unfriendly" behavior. Moreover, managers who are more oriented toward accepting the task orientation of established authority--demonstrating value sets focusing on conservative, established, correct ways of doing things--will likely display more friendly behavior. Managers who have value sets that are more oriented toward opposing task orientation of established authority--demonstrating value sets focusing on change to new procedures, different values, and creativity--will likely display more unfriendly behavior.

The P-N (Positive-Negative) dimension of behavior scores can be predicted by Marital status. This suggests that married managers are friendlier than single managers. Moreover, single managers are more unfriendly.

The implications for application suggest that senior managers and boards of governors should consider their hiring criteria. If a friendlier manager is desirable for the club, consider hiring a manager who is married. If a less friendly manager is desirable, consider hiring a single manager.

Behavior F-B

Table 7: Behavior F-B Model Summary

Model	R	R Square	Adjusted R Square	Std. Error of the Estimate
1	.617[a]	.381	.368	2.5897

a. Predictors: (Constant), Number of Members, Interaction Term V_UD*V_FB, Member Owned or Other, Values PN, Values FB, Values UD

Table 8: Behavior F-B ANOVA

Model		Sum of Squares	df	Mean Square	F	Sig.
1	Regression	1212.799	6	202.133	30.139	.000 [a]
	Residual	1971.762	294	6.707		
	Total	3184.561	300			

a.
Predictors: (Constant), Number of Members, Interaction Term V_UD*V_FB, Member Owned or Other, Values PN, Values FB, Values UD

Table 9: Behavior F-B Coefficients

Model		Unstandardized Coefficients		Standardized Coefficients		
		B	Std. Error	Beta	t	Sig.
1	(Constant)	.821	.562		1.460	.145
	Values UD	.546	.098	.396	5.551	.000
	Values PN	-.130	.042	-.149	-3.140	.002
	Values FB	.583	.051	.630	11.357	.000
	Interaction Term V_UD*V_FB	-6.305E-02	.015	-.324	-4.092	.000
	Member Owned or Other	.828	.387	.099	2.140	.033
	Number of Members	.167	.074	.104	2.256	.025

The F-B (Forward-Backward) dimension of behavior scores can be predicted by the U-D (Up-Down) dimension of values. This suggests that manager scores on the U dimensional element defined as "values on dominance" or the D dimensional element defined as "values on submissiveness" will reflect a positive relationship with the F dimensional element defined as "instrumentally controlled" behavior or the B dimensional element defined as "emotionally expressive" behavior. Moreover, managers who have value sets, which are more dominant, will be more instrumentally controlled. Managers who have value sets, which are more submissive, will be more emotionally expressive.

The F-B (Forward-Backward) dimension of behavior scores can be predicted by the P-N (Positive-Negative) dimension of values. This suggests that manager scores on the P dimensional element defined as "values on friendly behavior" or the N dimensional element defined as "values on unfriendly behavior" will reflect an inverse relationship with the F dimensional element defined as "instrumentally controlled" behavior or the B dimensional element defined as "emotionally expressive" behavior. Moreover, managers who have value sets, which are more positive--oriented toward values on friendly behavior, equality, and democratic participation in decision making--will be more emotionally expressive. Managers who are more negative--oriented toward values on unfriendly behavior, self-protection, self-interest first, and self-sufficiency--will be more instrumentally controlled.

The F-B (Forward-Backward) dimension of behavior scores can be predicted by the F-B dimension of values. This suggests that manager scores on the F dimensional element defined as "values on accepting task orientation of established authority" or the B dimensional element defined as "values on opposing task orientation of established authority" will reflect a positive relationship with scores on the F dimensional element defined as "instrumentally controlled" behavior or the B dimensional element defined as "emotionally expressive" behavior. Moreover, managers who have value sets oriented toward accepting task orientation of established authority--conservative, established, and correct ways of doing things--will be more instrumentally controlled. Managers who have value sets, which are more oriented toward opposing task orientation of established authority--change to new procedures, different values, and creativity--will be more emotionally expressive.

The F-B (Forward-Backward) dimension of behavior scores can be predicted by the interaction term V_U-D*V_F-B. This suggests that at any particular values U-D level, there is a positive relationship between the interaction with values F-B in predicting the F-B dimension of behavior. This suggests that the interaction of managers who have more dominant values and who demonstrate values on accepting task orientation of established authority would also likely exhibit behavior that is more emotionally expressive.

The implications for application suggest that senior managers and boards of governors should carefully examine their hiring practices. If, for example, a more dominant manager is identified who also demonstrates more values on accepting task orientation of established authority, the corresponding behavior will be more emotionally expressive. On the other hand, if a more submissive manager is identified, who also demonstrates more values on opposing task orientation of established authority, the finding suggests that the manager's behavior will be more instrumentally controlled.

The F-B (Forward-Backward) dimension of behavior scores can be predicted by type of ownership. This suggests that managers whose clubs are owned by the members are more instrumentally controlled. Moreover, managers whose clubs are owned by corporations, developers, individuals, or others are more emotionally expressive.

The implications for application suggest that senior managers and boards of governors should carefully examine the perceived fit when hiring a manager who is crossing over from a member-owned club to a corporate-owned club or vice versa. Managers from member-owned clubs are likely to keep their emotional arousal more closely in check, while managers from corporate-owned clubs feel freer to express their feelings. It is reasonable to suggest that due to these attributes, the move by a manager from a corporate-owned to member-owned club may be a more difficult transition than from member-owned to corporate-owned club.

The F-B (Forward-Backward) dimension of behavior scores can be predicted by number of members. This suggests that managers at clubs that have fewer members are more emotionally expressive. Moreover, managers at clubs that have more members are more instrumentally controlled.

Again, the implications for application suggest that senior managers and boards of governors should carefully examine the perceived fit when hiring a manager who is crossing over from a club with fewer members to a club with more members or vice versa. Managers from clubs with fewer members feel freer to express their feelings. Managers from clubs with more members are likely to keep their emotional arousal more closely in check. Due to these attributes, it is reasonable to suggest that the move by a manager from club with fewer members may be a more difficult transition than from a club with more members.

Limitations

The goal of this study was to detect relationships that might exist among the independent and dependent variables. Therefore, the nature of the study was classified as correlational instead of causal (Tuckman, 1998) and the type of study suggested a one-shot or one-time investigation correlational survey design instead of an experimental design (Campbell & Stanley, 1963). The study design therefore, can only suggest bases for correlational relationships that may exist.

This was the first time that leader values and behavior had been studied in this fashion. Therefore, conducting this study opens a research stream for organizational behavior. Additional studies in this area of organizational behavior would have helped suggest hypothesized relationships more precisely. Furthermore, this study included 301 managers from across the six geographic regions. Additional participants may have added to the validity of the findings.

The nature of this study as being cross-sectional rather than longitudinal may also be viewed as a limitation. However, the job at hand was examining leader values and behavior at one point--the situation--as described by Bales (1999). Moreover, as suggested by Merritt (1995), almost one half (44 percent) of leaders planned on leaving their present jobs within three years. (Note: This study found that almost one third [32.9 percent] of leaders surveyed planned on leaving their present jobs within three years.) Therefore, concern arose about erosion of sample size due to turnover. Concern also existed about managers' willingness to participate in multiple versions of the study over time, as was suggested during the club visits.

Significant differences between how the direct reports rated their managing supervisors and how the managing supervisors rated themselves were found. Future research could investigate this gap from the perspective of management development. This could be of benefit to senior managers who counsel managers in the employee review process.

This study included managers from six geographic areas included in the CMAA regions. However, expansion of CMAA's boundaries to include an international chapter of clubs and interest in international expansion by corporate-owned clubs suggests a possibility for future study. It might also prove interesting to study the relationships of values to behavior from a cultural perspective. For example, managers from the present study could be compared to international managers--ex-patriots from the U.S. and home-country managers outside the U.S.

Furthermore, these findings suggested in the present study beg the question: Will these findings hold across other sectors of the hospitality industry such as hotels and resorts, restaurants, and contract management? A next logical step could be to replicate the present study to the hotel industry and compare findings between industries.

Concluding Remarks

This study achieved two significant purposes: First, it enabled us to gain insight into leader values and how these values relate to behavior. In doing so, to the findings contribute to the stream of literature and further gusset the foundation of Bales' theory. Second, the findings fulfill many formative steps toward developing a model that integrates values, behavior, and—as moderators—demographic variables. Ultimately, these findings represent yet another small step at understanding human behavior in the workplace.

References

Bachman, W. (1988). Nice guys finish first: A SYMLOG analysis of U.S. naval commands. In R.B. Polley, A.P. Hare, & P.J. Stone (Eds.), *The SYMLOG practitioner: Applications of small group research* (pp.133-153). New York: Praeger.

Bales, R. (1970). *Personality and Interpersonal Behavior.* New York City: Holt, Rinehart, and Winston, Inc.

Bales, R. (1985). The new field theory in social psychology. *International Journal of Small Group Research*, 1, 1-18.

Bales, R. (1988). A new overview of the SYMLOG system. In R.B. Polley, A.P. Hare, & P.J. Stone (Eds.), *The SYMLOG practitioner: Applications of small group research* (pp. 319-344). New York: Praeger.

Bales, R. (1999). *Social interaction systems, theory and measurement.* New Brunswick, NJ: Transaction Press.

Bales, R., & Cohen, S. (1979). *SYMLOG: A system for the multiple level observation of groups.* New York: The Free Press.

Bales, R, & Isenberg, D. (1980). SYMLOG and leadership theory. In J.G. Hunt, U. Sekaran, & C.A. Schriesheim (Eds.),

Leadership: Beyond establishment views (pp. 165-195). Carbondale, IL: Southern Illinois University Press.

Bronowski, J. (1956). *Science and human values.* New York: Harper & Row.

Campbell, D, & Stanley, J. (1963). *Experimental and quasi-experimental designs for research.* Chicago: Rand McNally College Publishing.

Cline, R. (1996). Hospitality 2000: A view to the millennium. *Lodging Hospitality* (August), 20-26.

Connor, P. & Becker, B. (1994). Personal values and management: What do we need to know and why don't we know more? *Journal of Management Inquiry*, March, 68.

Coyle, M., & Dale, B. (1993). Quality in the hospitality industry: A study. *International Journal of Hospitality Management*, 12, 141-153.

Elizur, D., Borg, I., Hunt, R., & Beck, L. (1991). The structure of work values: A cross cultural comparison. *Journal of Organizational Behavior*, 12, 21-38.

Feather, N. (1992). Values, valences, expectations, and actions. *Journal of Social Issues*, 48 (2), 109-124.

Hofstede, G. (1980). *Culture's consequences: International differences in work-related values.* Beverly Hills, CA: Sage.

Hofstede, G. (1991). *Cultures and organizations: Software of the mind.* London, UK: McGraw-Hill.

Hogan, D. (1988). The SYMLOG leadership profile as a predictor of managerial performance. In R.B. Polley, A.P. Hare, & P.J. Stone (Eds.), *The SYMLOG practitioner* (pp. 191-210). New York: Praeger.

Kluckhohn F., & Strodtbeck, F. (1961). *Variations in value orientations.* Evanston, IL: Row Peterson.

Koenigs, R., & Cowen, M. (1988). SYMLOG as action research. In R.B. Polley, A.P. Hare, & P.J. Stone (Eds.), *The SYMLOG practitioner: applications of small group research* (pp. 61-87). New York: Praeger.

Lewin, K. (1951). *Field theory in social science.* New York: Harper and Row.

McClelland, D. (1980). Motive dispositions: The merits of operant and respondent measures. In L. Wheeler (Ed.), *Review of Personality and Social Psychology*, 1, 10-41.

McDougall, W. (1918). *Social psychology*. Boston: John W. Luce.

Merritt, E. (1995). *Hospitality management: A study of burnout in private club management*. Master's thesis: Pepperdine University, Malibu, CA.

Reber, A. (1995). *The penguin dictionary of psychology* (2nd ed.). New York: Penguin Books.

Schwartz, S. (1996). Value priorities and behavior: Applying a theory of integrated value systems. In C. Seligman, J. M. Olson, & M. P. Zanna (Eds.), *The psychology of values: The Ontario symposium* (Vol. 8, pp. 1-24). Mahwah, NJ: Lawrence Erlbaum.

Triandis, H. (1989). The self and social behavior in differing cultural contexts. *Psychological Review*, 96, 506-520.

Tuckman, B. (1998). *Conducting Educational Research*. New York: Harcourt Brace Jovanovich.

Yukl, G. (1998). *Leadership in organizations* (4th ed.). Englewood Cliffs, NJ: Prentice-Hall.

Article 02:

Burnout in Private Club Management

Article author: Edward A. Merritt

Summary

Club management is a difficult segment of the hospitality industry because of the emotional energy it consumes. The continuous amount of social effort required by managers represents extensive amounts of emotional labor. There is a high degree of mental and psychological work involved in treating every person and situation as individually important.

When managers reach the point of being used up and burned-out from too much emotional labor, their hearts are no longer in their work. Quality begins to slip. The staff and members react negatively to such a downturn, which further exacerbates a difficult situation.

As demonstrated by the results of this study, many managers suffer high levels of burnout working their way to the top. However, successfully reaching the top—becoming a general manager—does not always create a significant drop in burnout.

Different types of responsibilities seem to function differently as stressors. One way to categorize this variable is responsibility for people versus responsibility for things. The effects of long-term stress can lead to burnout and turnover.

According to Maslach, burnout is a multidimensional construct of emotional exhaustion, depersonalization, and reduced personal accomplishment that can occur among individuals who work extensively with others under considerable time pressures. Furthermore, burnout is particularly relevant to individuals when working with people in emotionally charged situations. From that reference, it seems likely that club managers are prime candidates for burnout.

Turnover is a major topic throughout this study for these reasons: Turnover is a major contributor to burnout for managers because of the constant need for recruiting and training of new workers. Moreover, turnover is often the result of what happens to managers after they become burned-out. Therefore, turnover is both a cause, and an effect of burnout. Hospitality turnover averages well over 100 percent annually as an industry. This means that employees stay on the job, on the average, about one year.

Turnover has become a more serious challenge recently as the supply of available workers has dwindled. As a result, the industry now finds itself filling jobs with almost anyone willing to work. Sometimes, jobs cannot be filled at all, further compounding the stress levels of managers.

This study includes the feelings of management staff of private clubs throughout the United States. Its purpose was to determine the demographics and other information that, when compared to the results a burnout inventory (The Maslach Burnout Inventory), identified a manager profile more susceptible to burnout than that of other managers.

The Maslach Burnout Inventory (MBI) is used to assess the three aspects of the burnout syndrome: Emotional Exhaustion, Depersonalization, and lack of Personal Accomplishment. Maslach contends that burnout exists in each of us by degrees. From that viewpoint, it seems that stress and burnout are more closely related than separate.

By Maslach's measures, high burnout is reflected in high scores in Emotional Exhaustion and Depersonalization and in low scores in Personal Accomplishment. Average burnout is reflected in average scores on the three subscales. Low burnout is reflected in low scores in Emotional Exhaustion and Depersonalization and in high scores in Personal Accomplishment. Maslach's overall averages of thousands of participants for the three measures are shown in the table that follows:

Overall Sample

	Low	Average	High
Emotional Exhaustion	≤16	17-26	≥27
Depersonalization	≤6	7-12	≥13
Personal Accomplishment	≥39	38-32	≤31

The Emotional Exhaustion question group for this study totaled 20.09—Average when compared to the Overall Categorization. Depersonalization scored 8.81 for the study, also Average. Personal Accomplishment also ranked Average range with 37.03.

Cross tabulating results of the Burnout Inventory by demographic selectors, the study identified both expected and unexpected findings. A summary of some of those findings follows:

Summary of Findings

- Clubhouse Managers are the single-most burned-out group.
- Golf Club Managers experience highest burnout; Athletic Club Managers, the least.
- Managers with less than 5 years in the club profession are the most burned-out. Managers with the most years in the industry are the least burned-out.
- Managers with the least amount of time at their clubs are most burned-out in each subscale.
- Managers that work the least amount of hours per week are the most burned-out. Those that work the most are the least burned-out.
- The youngest Managers rate far above anyone else in burnout. The oldest Managers show the least burnout.
- Men are considerably more burned-out than women.
- Managers from the North experience more burnout than anyone else. Managers from the West experience the least.

- Single, Previously Married Managers exhibit the lowest burnout; Married Managers exhibit the most.
- Managers planning to stay at their clubs less than 1 year are the most burned-out.
- Managers with the fewest members are the most burned-out; Managers with the most members are the least.
- Managers at clubs not performing well are the most burned-out. Managers reporting club performance as better than in past show the lowest amount.
- Managers predicting the industry as doing worse than in past are the most burned-out. Managers expecting it to do better are the least.
- Managers predicting their clubs will do better than in past show the least amount of burnout. Managers predicting worse, show the most.

The growth in numbers of private clubs creates an increase in need for more and effective managers. Boards of governors and senior managers that supervise private club managers should understand burnout's causes and effects. However, identifying and documenting problems alone does not lead to solutions—it serves instead as an important first step. From there, boards and senior managers must examine data to isolate factors that contribute to burnout, and develop a plan to reduce or eliminate such factors.

Introduction

Dealing with members and employees is different from solitary work where you are developing ideas, working with numbers, or operating equipment. To manage a club effectively, you must be visible and engaged. You work with expectations and misunderstandings. You deal with personalities—you must cope with their frustrations. It can be difficult, and therefore, stressful.

Physical Versus Mental Labor

Some jobs are difficult because of the physical labor involved. People must move things or perpetually be on the go.

Some of this activity is involved in managing clubs. But that is not the answer to why managing is difficult. Club management is challenging because of the emotional energy it consumes. The intangible quality of communicating with and working well with people—the social effort—consumes an extensive amount of emotional labor.

Managers must greet people constantly and enthusiastically; and they must serve and please. Managers must treat people as special. There is a great deal of mental and psychological work involved in treating every person and every situation as being individually important.

Working with people can be gratifying when it all goes well. However, a manager still must invest great amounts of energy into such a process. The emotional expenditure is much greater when people become uncooperative. Dealing with these situations requires physical stamina; in addition, such situations test a manager's psychological stamina. Eventually, it can lead to emotional fatigue.

When managers reach the point of being burned-out from too much emotional labor, it shows in their work. Quality begins to slip. The staff and members react negatively to such a downturn, which creates an even more difficult situation. It can become a vicious cycle where everyone loses—the manager, the club, and the member or employee. To a large degree, members measure the quality of a club by the quality of service. In their eyes, the managers and staff are the organization. A manager helps shape that reputation every day. That amount of responsibility can be exhilarating in the sense that a manager has great flexibility to orchestrate a successful operation. On the other hand, it can also become a negative reflection upon that same manager when the club fails to meet member expectations.

Changing population demographics are causing hospitality organizations to place more emphasis on employee retention and productivity than ever before. As the availability of labor dwindles, the focus is on organizational climate. Clubs need to know that there is a direct relationship between employee withdrawal (including turnover, absenteeism, and burnout) and job satisfaction.[1] As demonstrated by the results of this study, many managers suffer high levels of burnout on their way to the top. Achievement of a general manager's position does not translate to a significant overall drop in feelings of burnout.

Stress and Burnout

Interest in burnout in the hospitality industry has become widespread in recent years. The demand for quick financial fixes, a nagging club president, low job security, and the constancy of working closely with people in difficult situations are some of the causes of such interest. Over time many managers leave clubs because they feel burned-out by the hectic pace.

During the past two decades, the term burnout has become commonplace. Burnout might be defined as psychological distress that may develop into physical illness when no relief appears to be forthcoming. Personal definitions of stress differ widely. The club manager may view stress as frustration; a pilot sees it as a problem of concentration; a biochemist thinks of it as a chemical event. Nelson and Quick define stress as the unconscious preparation to fight or flee a person experiences when faced with any demand.[2] A variety of dissimilar situations—work effort, fatigue, uncertainty, fear, or emotional arousal—are capable of producing stress. Therefore, to isolate a single factor as the sole cause of stress is extremely difficult.

Past Studies

Burnout is perhaps easier to observe than to define. In an effort to define burnout, one author offered these insightful comments:

> Billions of dollars are lost each year . . . because of workers who can no longer function in, or cope successfully with, their jobs. More than just the monetary loss . . . is the loss suffered by the people in the process. In recent years the signs and symptoms of these problems, i.e., turnover, absenteeism, lowered productivity, psychological problems, etc., have become increasingly predominant in our society. . . . To attempt to define the condition itself is difficult. . . . This condition

... can be defined as all of those ... problems on the job that result in a negative interface between individuals and environments as people attempt to adapt within the organization.[3]

Freudenberger was the first to use the term burnout to denote a state of physical and emotional depletion that results from conditions of work.[4] Maslach used the term to describe an over-extension of self that evolves into a severe loss of energy and deterioration in performance.[5]

According to Maslach, burnout is a multidimensional construct of emotional exhaustion, depersonalization, and reduced personal accomplishment that can occur among individuals who work extensively with others under considerable time pressures.[6] From that reference, it seems club managers are prime candidates for burnout.

A key aspect of the burnout syndrome is increased feelings of emotional exhaustion; as emotional resources are depleted, workers feel they are no longer able to give of themselves at a psychological level. Another aspect of the burnout syndrome is the development of depersonalization—i.e., negative, cynical attitudes and feelings about one's clients. . . . The development of depersonalization appears to be related to the experience of emotional exhaustion, and so these two aspects should be corrected. A third aspect of the burnout syndrome, a feeling of reduced personal accomplishments, refers to the tendency to evaluate oneself negatively, particularly with regard to one's work with clients. Workers may feel unhappy about themselves and dissatisfied with their accomplishments on the job.7

Burnout, as studied by those early researchers, was assumed to be particularly relevant to individuals whose work focused on working with people in emotionally charged situations. Later, studies involving a psychological profile frequently represented in managerial occupations found that burnout was also associated with increased mental demands.[8] It seems the dimensions of the burnout described in these two types of job situations are different.

Statement of The Problem

Burnout leads to substantial direct and indirect business operating costs.[9] The consequences of burnout are potentially dangerous for the staff, the members, and the clubs in which they work.[10] Research of Lang; Reynolds and Tabacchi; and Krone, Tabacchi, and Farber reveals that other hospitality-industry managers experience destructive feelings that should be addressed. It was clear the subject of burnout warranted further investigation.

About the Study

The Research Question

What is the sample profile of the most, down to the least burned out club manager?

Purpose

The purpose of the burnout study is to rank the variables identified in focus groups to compare to the burnout instrument, and thereby create a sample profile to determine the most, down to the least burned-out manager. This study reveals the results of the survey and documents what managers had to say about the effects of burnout. Additionally, the survey, through cross tabulation, is interpreted as to its possible meanings and ramifications. Finally, insight gained during personal interviews, comments, and conversations is shared with the reader, as are recommendations that can be implemented to reduce burnout in private clubs.

Participants

This study was conducted among management-level staff working at private clubs. Typical position titles include General Manager, Manager, Clubhouse Manager, and Assistant Manager. One hundred fifty-two managers (n=152) of private clubs throughout the United States participated in the study. The survey was conducted by mail with a three-part instrument including demographic and descriptive information, the Maslach

Burnout Inventory, and one optional, open-ended question soliciting comments about successes or challenges of club management.

Demographics

The demographic and descriptive information component of the survey contains 14 variables:

1. Job title.
2. Type of club.
3. Years in club management.
4. Years at their present club.
5. Hours worked.
6. Age.
7. Gender.
8. In which of five areas of the country they were located.
9. Marital Status.
10. Length of time they plan to stay at their club.
11. Number of members.
12. Club performance over the past year.
13. Expectation for industry performance over the coming year.
14. Expectation for club performance over the coming year.

The demographic and descriptive information statements were developed from small focus-group studies and telephone conversations conducted during spring 1995. The focus groups included a total of 25 participants composed of managers, hospitality educators, and association executives. During the sessions, participants were asked open-ended questions to loosely-guide the subject matter. However, the focus-group sessions were allowed to develop on their own to uncover areas of importance. For example, the following question began each session: "How do you feel when you hear the subject of burnout mentioned?" Following the focus-group sessions, educators and association executives responded to direct questions. For example, "After reading the list of questions proposed from focus-group studies, please make suggestions for additional questions or modifications." The idea was to use the educators and association executives as editors in finalizing and smoothing questions, and to clarify answers.

Burnout Inventory Instrumentation

Along with the completion of demographic and descriptive information, respondent managers were asked to comment on 22 statements regarding their feelings and attitudes about burnout—The Maslach Burnout Inventory (MBI). The survey instrument instructed them to mark the selection that most-closely indicated their feelings on a Likert-type scale answer grid (0 = Never, 6 = Every day).

Burnout can lead to deterioration in the quality of service provided by the staff. It appears to be a factor in job turnover, absenteeism, and low morale. Furthermore, burnout seems to be correlated with various self-reported indices of personal dysfunction, including physical exhaustion, insomnia, increased use of alcohol and drugs, and marital and family problems. The generally consistent pattern of findings that emerged from this research led . . . to an instrument to assess it. This measure, the Maslach Burnout Inventory (MBI), contains three subscales that assess the different aspects of experienced burnout. It has been found to be reliable, valid, and easy to administer.[11]

The MBI has been validated as a reliable tool for measuring burnout, and has been used many times within the hospitality industry.[12] Maslach views burnout as a combination of three factors or dimensions: depersonalization, emotional exhaustion, and the lack of personal accomplishment. Accordingly, the Maslach Burnout Inventory (MBI) rates people on these three subscales (dimensions) by determining how people respond to each of 22 statements. Respondents state the frequency of such feelings, ranging from never to every day. The higher the respondents score on depersonalization and emotional exhaustion, the higher their levels of burnout. The lack of personal accomplishment scale measures in the opposite direction. That is, the lower the scale, the higher the burnout level. A list of the questions from the MBI is provided below:

1. I feel emotionally drained from my work.
2. I feel used up at the end of the work day.

3. I feel fatigued when I get up in the morning and have to face another day on the job.
4. I can easily understand how people I work with feel about things.
5. I feel I treat some people in an impersonal manner.
6. Working with people all day is a strain for me.
7. I deal very effectively with problems people bring me at work.
8. I feel burned-out from my work.
9. I feel I am making a difference in other people's lives through my work.
10. I've become more callous toward people since I took this job.
11. I worry that this job is hardening me emotionally.
12. I feel very energetic.
13. I feel frustrated by my job.
14. I feel I'm working too hard on my job.
15. I don't really care what happens to some people I encounter at work.
16. Working with people directly puts too much stress on me.
17. I can easily create a relaxed atmosphere with people at work.
18. I feel exhilarated after working with people closely on my job.
19. I have accomplished many worthwhile things in this job.
20. I feel like I'm at the end of my rope.
21. In my work, I deal with emotional problems very calmly.
22. I feel others at work blame me for some of their problems.

Open-Ended Question

The final component of the survey instrument included one open-ended question that encouraged managers to write about successes or challenges in their work. The statement at the end of the survey states, "Please attach an additional sheet if you would like to share any challenges or successes of working in the private club industry."

Measuring Tools

The authors used Microsoft Excel® and Minitab® to analyze answers, counts, and averages, and cross-tabulation to draw relationships among demographic components and burnout.

About the Study Participants

Sample Selection, Strategy, and Procedures

Addresses for survey participants were obtained from the Club Managers Association of America Yearbook. An equal number of survey recipients was selected from 50 of the 51 CMAA Chapter Cross References. Due to distance, unreliable mail delivery, and high postage costs, the Far East Chapter was excluded. The study included the 48 contiguous States, plus Alaska and Hawaii. A total of 316 individually-addressed envelopes were posted with first-class stamps and mailed. Managers were asked to complete and return the survey within 30 days.

In addition to the primary survey, a second survey was enclosed in each envelope requesting that managers ask one of their senior assistants to fill-out and return a survey to help broaden the sample of the industry.

Respondents

Of the respondent base of 152 managers, the job title profile includes General Managers (61 percent), Managers (13 percent), Clubhouse Managers (10 percent), Assistant Managers (9 percent), and Other management-level staff members (7 percent).

A variety of types of private clubs are represented in the survey. Country Clubs represent the majority in the club-type affiliation category at 70.9 percent, followed by City Clubs (12.6 percent), and Golf (8.6 percent). Minor club categories round out the profile with Yacht Clubs (2.6 percent), Athletic Clubs (1.3 percent), and Other types of clubs (4 percent).

The majority of the respondents have worked many years in the club profession. The profile of managers in the survey on the number of years worked in the industry includes 10-15 years

(29 percent), 5-10 years (26 percent), 15-20 years (17 percent), more than 20 years (16 percent), and less than 5 years (12 percent).

The largest percentage of managers in the survey have worked at their present club more than 7 years (33.1 percent). The remainder of the profile in order from most to least, includes 1-3 years (27.2 percent), a tie in the categories of 3-5 years and 5-7 years (16.6 percent), and less than 1 year (6.6 percent).

Manager respondents help corroborate the industry reputation for long work hours. Almost half work 50-60 hours per week. An astounding 80.7 percent of the sample work between 50-70 hours each week or more. The manager profile for the survey includes 50-60 hours (47.3 percent), 60-70 hours (28.7 percent), 40-50 hours (19.3 percent), and more than 70 hours (4.7 percent). Although listed as a possible answer, no manager selected less than 40 hours per week.

As expected, the majority of managers (approximately 70 percent) in the survey range from 30-50 years of age. The manager profile includes 30-40 years old (35.8 percent), 40-50 (33.8 percent), more than 50 (18.5 percent), 25-30 (7.9 percent), and less than 25 (4 percent).

Male respondents outnumber female respondents by a wide margin, but in keeping with the demographics of the mailing list itself. The gender profile includes male (86 percent) and female (14 percent).

The geographic location tabulation divides the country into five regions: North (27 percent), South (26 percent), Central (23 percent), West (17 percent), and drops off sharply with Mountain representing just 7 percent of the sample.

The overwhelming percentage of respondents in the survey sample are married. The marital status profile includes Married (76.8 percent), Never Married (11.9 percent), and Single, Previously Married (11.3 percent). For clarification, the category Married includes those managers that are presently married, although they may have been previously divorced.

Managers vary in their answers on how much longer they plan to stay at their present club. The most frequently chosen option is a disappointing 1-3 years (30.6 percent), followed by more than 7 years (25.2 percent), 3-5 years (21.8 percent), less than 1 year (13.6 percent), and 5-7 years (8.8 percent). When combining the 1-3 year group with the less than 1 year group, it is significant to note that more than 44 percent of managers plan to leave their present job within 3 years.

Over half the clubs in the sample have memberships of more than 600 members (57 percent), followed by 500-599 (20 percent), 400-499 (12 percent), 300-399 (7 percent), and finally the classically envisioned club of less than 300 members representing a mere 4 percent of the survey.

Club performance over the past year is improved for 65.5 percent of the respondents, followed by same as in past (20.5 percent), and worse than in past (13.9 percent).

Managers are optimistic in their expectations for the industry over the next 12 months. 43.7 percent expect the industry to perform better than in the past, followed by same as in past (40.4 percent), and worse than in past selected by just 15.9 percent.

Similar to past club performance and feelings about future industry performance, managers believe their clubs will improve in the coming 12 months. 69.5 percent predict better than in past, 20.5 percent say it will be the same as in past, and a low 9.9 percent predict worse than in past.

Typical Respondent

1.	Job title:	General Manager.
2.	Working at a:	Country Club.
3.	Has been in profession:	10-15 years.
4.	Has been at present club:	More than seven years.
5.	Works:	50-60 hours per week.
6.	Age:	30-40 years old.
7.	Gender:	Male.
8.	Presently works in the:	Northern part of the country.
9.	Marital status:	Married.
10.	Plans to stay at present club:	1-3 more years.
11.	Manages at a club with a membership:	More than 600 members.

12. Club performance over past 12 months:	Better than in past.
13. Expectations for industry over next 12 months:	Better than in past.
14. Expectations for club over next 12 months:	Better than in past.

Aspects

In this study, the Maslach Burnout Inventory (MBI)[13] is used to assess the three aspects of the burnout syndrome identified by Maslach: Emotional Exhaustion, Depersonalization, and lack of Personal Accomplishment. Each aspect is then measured by a separate subscale. The Emotional Exhaustion subscale measures feelings of emotional over-extension and work exhaustion. The Depersonalization subscale measures an unfeeling and impersonal response toward club members, employees, or others. The Personal Accomplishment subscale measures feelings of competence and successful achievement in a manager's work with people.[14] Respondent managers selected one answer out of a possible six for each of 22 statements.

Burnout: A Continuous Variable

Maslach considers burnout a continuous variable, ranging from low to average (moderate) to high degrees of experienced feeling. In her opinion, burnout is not viewed as a variable that is either present or absent. From that viewpoint, it seems the words stress and burnout become more related than with the more popular lay reference to a condition of burnout developing at some imprecise point after experiencing periods of long-term stress.

Scores are considered high if they are in the upper third of the normative distribution, average if they are in the middle third, and low if they are in the lower third. Furthermore, according to Maslach, given limited knowledge about the relationship between the three aspects of burnout, the scores for each subscale are considered separately and are not combined into a single, total score. Thus, three scores are computed for each respondent.[15]

Aspect Measuring

Emotional Exhaustion

The range of experienced burnout for this survey overall in Emotional Exhaustion is 20.09—Average when compared to the Overall Categorization of MBI Scores.

Depersonalization

The range of experienced burnout for this survey overall in Depersonalization is 8.81—Average when compared to the Overall Categorization of MBI Scores.

Personal Accomplishment

The range of experienced burnout for this survey overall in Personal Accomplishment is 37.03—Average when compared to the Overall Categorization of MBI Scores.

Findings

The next step of this study is to identify the profile of the most, down to the least burned-out manager in the survey based on demographics and other facts. Findings are presented as charts in the appendix.

Highest Burnout From Emotional Exhaustion

1.	Job title:	Clubhouse Manager.
2.	Working at a:	Golf Club.
3.	Has been in the club profession:	Less than 5 years.
4.	Has been at present club:	Less than 1 year.
5.	Works:	40-50 hours per week.
6.	Age:	Less than 25 years old.

7.	Gender:	Male.
8.	Presently works in the:	Northern part of the country.
9.	Marital status:	Married.
10.	Plans to stay at present club:	Less than 1 year.
11.	Manages at a club with a membership:	Less than 300 members.
12.	Club performance over past 12 months:	Worse than in past.
13.	Expectations for industry over next 12 months:	Worse than in past.
14.	Expectations for club over next 12 months:	Worse than in past.

Lowest Burnout From Emotional Exhaustion

The theoretical club manager respondent for the survey experiencing the lowest degree of burnout from Emotional Exhaustion displays the following characteristics:

1.	Job title:	Assistant Manager.
2.	Working at an:	Athletic Club.
3.	Has been in the club profession:	More than 20 years.
4.	Has been at present club:	5-7 years.
5.	Works:	More than 70 hours per week.
6.	Age:	More than 50 years old.
7.	Gender:	Female.
8.	Presently works in the:	Western part of the country.
9.	Marital status:	Single, previously married.
10.	Plans to stay at present club:	More than 7 years.
11.	Manages at a club with a membership:	More than 600 members.

12. Club performance over past 12 months:	Better than in past.
13. Expectations for industry over next 12 months:	Better than in past.
14. Expectations for club over next 12 months:	Better than in past.

Highest Burnout From Depersonalization

The theoretical club manager respondent for the survey that demonstrates the highest degree of burnout from Depersonalization has these attributes:

1. Job title:	General Manager.
2. Working at a:	Golf Club.
3. Has been in the club profession:	Less than 5 years.
4. Has been at present club:	Less than 1 year.
5. Works:	40-50 hours per week.
6. Age:	Less than 25 years old.
7. Gender:	Male.
8. Presently works in the:	Northern part of the country.
9. Marital status:	Married.
10. Plans to stay at present club:	Less than 1 year.
11. Manages at a club with a membership:	Less than 300 members.
12. Club performance over past 12 months:	Worse than in past.
13. Expectations for industry over next 12 months:	Worse than in past.
14. Expectations for club over next 12 months:	Worse than in past.

Lowest Burnout From Depersonalization

The theoretical club manager respondent for the survey indicating the lowest degree of burnout from Depersonalization looks like this:

1.	Job title:	Other Manager.
2.	Working at an:	Athletic Club.
3.	Has been in the club profession:	More than 20 years.
4.	Has been at present club:	More than 7 years.
5.	Works:	More than 70 hours per week.
6.	Age:	More than 50 years old.
7.	Gender:	Female.
8.	Presently works in the:	Western part of the country.
9.	Marital status:	Single, previously married.
10.	Plans to stay at present club:	More than 7 years.
11.	Manages at a club with a membership:	More than 600 members.
12.	Club performance over past 12 months:	Better than in past.
13.	Expectations for industry over next 12 months:	Better than in past.
14.	Expectations for club over next 12 months:	Better than in past.

Highest Burnout From Personal Accomplishment (Lack Of)

The theoretical club manager respondent for the survey enduring the highest degree of burnout from Personal Accomplishment has these characteristics:

1.	Job title:	General Manager.
2.	Working at a:	Golf Club.

3.	Has been in the club profession:	Less than 5 years.
4.	Has been at present club:	Less than 1 year.
5.	Works:	40-50 hours per week.
6.	Age:	Less than 25 years old.
7.	Gender:	Male.
8.	Presently works in the:	Northern part of the country.
9.	Marital status:	Married.
10.	Plans to stay at present club:	Less than 1 year.
11.	Manages at a club with a membership:	Less than 300 members.
12.	Club performance over past 12 months:	Worse than in past.
13.	Expectations for industry over next 12 months:	Worse than in past.
14.	Expectations for club over next 12 months:	Worse than in past.

Lowest Burnout From Personal Accomplishment (Lack Of)

Finally, the theoretical club manager respondent for the survey scoring the lowest degree of burnout from Personal Accomplishment has these characteristics:

1.	Job title:	Other Manager.
2.	Working at an:	Athletic Club.
3.	Has been in the club profession:	More than 20 years.
4.	Has been at present club:	More than 7 years.
5.	Works:	More than 70 hours per week.
6.	Age:	More than 50 years old.
7.	Gender:	Female.
8.	Presently works in the:	Western part of the country.

9. Marital status:	Single, previously married.
10. Plans to stay at present club:	3-5 years.
11. Manages at a club with a membership:	More than 600 members.
12. Club performance over past 12 months:	Better than in past.
13. Expectations for industry over next 12 months:	Better than in past.
14. Expectations for club over next 12 months:	Better than in past.

Implications

This study identified a number of both expected and unexpected findings regarding burnout in the private club segment of the hospitality industry. What follows is a summary of some of those findings:

- Clubhouse Managers are highest in burnout by each measure: Emotional Exhaustion, Depersonalization, and Personal Accomplishment.
- Golf Club Managers experience highest levels of burnout—by far—than others; Athletic Club Managers, the least.
- Managers with less than 5 years in the club profession are more burned-out than any other group. Managers with the most years in the business are the least burned-out.
- Managers with the least amount of time at their clubs are most burned-out in each subscale.
- Managers that work the least amount of hours per week are the most burned-out. Those that work the most are the least burned-out.
- The youngest Managers rate far above anyone else in burnout. The oldest Managers show the least burnout.
- Men are considerably more burned-out than women.

- Managers from the North experience more burnout than anyone else. Managers from the West experience the least.
- Single, Previously Married Managers exhibit the lowest burnout; Married Managers the most.
- Managers planning to stay at their clubs less than 1 year are the most burned-out.
- Managers with the fewest members are the most burned-out; Managers with the most members are the least.
- Managers at clubs not performing well are also the most burned-out. Managers reporting club performance as better show the lowest amount.
- Managers predicting the industry as doing worse than in past are the most burned-out. Managers expecting it to do better are the least.
- Managers predicting their clubs will do better than in past show the least amount of burnout. Managers predicting worse show the most.

Recommendations

The growth in numbers of private clubs creates an increase in need for more and effective managers. Boards of governors and senior managers that supervise private club managers should understand burnout's causes and effects. However, identifying and documenting problems alone does not lead to solutions—it serves instead as an important first step. From there, boards and senior managers must examine data to isolate factors that contribute to burnout, and develop a plan to reduce or eliminate such factors.

From the findings of this study, examining other research findings, and interviewing other managers, the authors propose the following recommendations to reduce factors that contribute to burnout:

- Examine the club culture. Vallen found that 20-30 percent of absenteeism and turnover is related to job dissatisfaction, involving either personal factors, the work environment, or job conflict. Burnout is often associated with the same factors.[16] It therefore makes good sense to examine your corporate culture and make changes if necessary.

- Ensure job descriptions are honest and clear. Reduce misunderstandings about duties and expectations.
- Motivate the entire staff (see table below).

--Challenge managers and staff	--Allow managers to fail without negative action
--Create meaningful incentive programs	--Establish mutually agreeable goals and objectives
--Rid the club of bureaucracy	--Flatten the organization's structure.
--Allow an open-door policy	--Communicate up and down throughout the club

- Encourage networking. Association and peer group networking opportunities help provide an outside support group atmosphere so that managers do not feel isolated and uninformed.
- Allow an informal, relaxed atmosphere. Encourage everyone to laugh and have fun at work.
- Weigh the extent of club policies and attitudes that encourage burnout. Change policies where appropriate.
- Create Employee Assistance Plans (EAPs). Club managers and staff work long and unusual schedules and do not always take time to strengthen personal and family relationships. Furthermore, the festive atmosphere and constant presence of alcohol can prove to be a difficult environment for those dealing with weaknesses, habits, and addictions. Programs such as those listed below, provide opportunities for employee retention (see table below).

--Day care	--Counseling	--Support groups
--Education	--Flexible benefits plans	--Employee retention plans such as retirement

--Stress management programs	--Time management programs	--Encourage exercise programs and regimens
--Wellness programs	--Financial planning	--Substance abuse programs

- Understand the lifestyle of a private club manager does not encourage socializing outside of work. Single managers often stay single or marry someone in the industry. Married managers can become pressured at home, especially when the spouse has a 'normal' job. Encourage creative work policies to help address these issues (see table below).

--Adopt a 5-day, 50-hour work week	--Allow managers one weekend per month off	--Allow 2 flex days per month in order to catch up
--Post schedules to allow for planning a personal life	--Grant compensatory time off after busy periods	--Tap into the non-traditional workforce

- Reduce role conflict.
- Ensure overall goals are mutually agreed upon—and that they are achievable.
- Emphasize overall results. Allow managers to do their jobs.
- Educate young managers about the challenges and realities of the industry. Ensure they do not develop unreasonable expectations. "The learning curve flattens significantly after a year or two. That is when management turnover problem really starts. The first year it is fun to beat the numbers; the second year, you beat your own; the third year is a real pain."[17]

- Reduce burnout and turnover substantially by keeping managers involved (see table below).[18]

--Club Managers Association continuing education	--Courses and training	--Promotions
--Feedback	--Allow them to vent frustrations	--Bottom-up thinking[19]

- Empower others to do their best. People want to work in an atmosphere where they are given the tools, responsibility, and support to get the job accomplished.[20]

Article 03:

Establishing and Managing Goals and Objectives

Article authors: Edward A. Merritt and Florence Berger

In Brief

Managers are expected to perform a multitude of functions including executing their responsibilities through others. They cannot expect to manage others if they cannot manage themselves. Establishing a system of goals is a valuable tool that will enable managers to manage themselves and others. Effective goal setting can provide managers with many benefits including: directing attention, encouraging high-level performance, developing innovation and persistence, and diminishing stress. The goal-setting process includes six steps: specify the goal and how to accomplish it, create a SMART goal, identify resources and risk involved, and obtain feedback. Two effective ways to approach goal achievement are through visualization and setting objectives. Once managers have established their goals and have moved toward achieving them, they can begin to coach their employees on goal setting. Effective methods of coaching include: staying in contact, praising, communicating the importance of the process, ensuring capability, allowing employees to reward and critique themselves, choosing the right time and method, publicizing goals, considering using negative feedback in a non-evaluative way, and mitigating conflict. For this paper, I interviewed 22 hospitality industry leaders (my expert panel) regarding their use of goal setting. Of these participants, only one said that he did not use principles of goal setting on a daily basis.

Statement of The Problem: Why Goal Setting?

When managers do not care where they are going, goals are not important. In Lewis Carroll's, Alice's Adventures in

Wonderland, Alice and the Cheshire Cat had the following conversation:

Alice: "Would you tell me, please, which way I ought to go from here?"

Cheshire Cat: "That depends a good deal on where you want to get to."

Alice: "I don't much care."

Cheshire Cat: "Then it doesn't matter which way you go."21

Goal setting is vital when managers want to know where they are going. The key to success for many senior-level managers is their ability not only to manage others but to discipline and manage themselves. Through this skill one is able to set realistic goals and objectives and determine the most efficient and effective way to achieve them. Continual goal setting and achievement helps assure continued success.

Managers are expected to perform a multitude of functions including planning, organizing, leading, and controlling, and perhaps most important, executing their responsibilities in a way that produces desired goals. Successful managers must be able to make efficient use of time, delegate responsibility to others, and be aware of both the long and short term effects of their decisions. Managers cannot expect to manage other people if they cannot use time wisely, complete tasks as scheduled, and provide leadership and direction to the employees they supervise. Establishing a system of goals is a valuable tool that will enable managers to do both—manage themselves and others.

The successes of Steve Wynn, then chairman and president of Mirage Resorts (named by Forbes Magazine in 1996 as one of America's 10 Most Admired Companies) and Rich Melman who has built his Lettuce Entertain You Enterprises into a $140-million empire in 25 years are probably familiar to you. Each enjoys success because of diligently pursued goals.

First, I will discuss some of the details of the study—including its purpose, methodology, findings, implications and lessons, and discuss an idea for a future study. Second, I introduce the subject of goal setting by discussing some of its many benefits identified by the study participants. The third section is devoted to the step process in establishing a goal: Problem identification, strategy mapping, setting a performance goal, identifying necessary resources, recognizing risk, and obtaining constructive feedback. The fourth section is a discussion of a variety of methods for goal achievement once the goal is established. The fifth and final section lists techniques managers can use in managing others through goal setting. If managers need an incentive to read further, remember that organizations that implement goal setting reap greater profits than organizations that do not.22 An astounding 100 percent of study participants state that goal setting increases their organizations' bottom lines by at least 10 percent.

About the Study
Purpose

The purpose of this study is to determine if the time and effort necessary to develop and implement a system of goal setting are beneficial to a hospitality organization's success. The expert panel overwhelmingly agrees that the time and effort are, indeed, beneficial and worth the trouble. In addition to asking if managers use goal setting, I asked those that answered "yes," to quantify the impact of such programs on their bottom lines. Given the strong findings in favor of a goal setting program, I then utilized respondent comments in developing a tool kit for managers to use in creating such a system.

Methodology

I contacted a stratified sample of 30 senior-level hospitality throughout the country to ask if they would participate in a qualitative study on goal setting. Of the 30 managers contacted, 22 (n=22) agreed to individual, in-depth interviews to help us probe further into the subject.

My assumption was that the positive results that could be derived from an effective system of goal setting and implementation are worth the effort in terms of increased bottom-line profit to the hospitality organizations. However, I wanted to find out from the panel if the benefits are worth the time and effort involved in developing and implementing such a program. Furthermore, assuming managers answered in the affirmative—that the benefits are worth the time and effort—I would use such information as the basis to help answer another question: How can hospitality managers develop and institute effective goal setting and implementation programs in their organizations?

Study Participants

This study was conducted among 22 (n=22) senior management staff working at hotels, resorts, private clubs, and restaurants across the United States. Typical position titles include Owner, Corporate Executive, District or Regional Manager, General Manager, and Manager. The interviews were conducted by telephone and mail.

Demographic Information

First, I asked the expert panel to tell us about themselves. The demographic and descriptive information component of the study contains six statements to determine answers to such variables as these:

- Job title.
- Length of time in the hospitality management profession.
- Length of time in present position.
- Age.
- Gender.
- In which of five areas of the country they live.

See appendix A for a breakdown of demographic information relative to the interview respondents.

Study Questions

Next, I asked the panel to tell us about their work. Participants were asked eight major questions to help guide the subject matter. However, interview sessions were allowed to develop on their own to uncover areas of importance. From those answers, extemporaneous focus questions were asked where appropriate to help clarify information provided:

- Amount of management functions performed. Note: The idea of this question is to determine a broad spectrum of general management responsibilities in the areas of planning, organizing, coordinating, and controlling, as opposed to the narrow focus of technical segment specialists.
- Number of direct reports.
- If they use goal setting.
- If yes, its effect on the organization's bottom line.
- Observed benefits of goal setting.
- Steps used to create goals—the process.
- Once goals are set, methods used for goal achievement.
- Techniques used in managing others through goal setting.

See appendix B for a synopsis of categorized information relative to this group of study questions.

Findings

Job title:
- 45% (10 individuals) of study participants hold the job title of general manager.
- 41% (9) of study participants hold a job title such as area manager or regional manager, corporate executive, or owner.
- 14% (3) of study participants hold the job title of manager.
- Years in hospitality profession:
- 41% (9) of study participants have been in the hospitality profession for 15 to 20 years.
- 36% (8) of study participants have been in the hospitality profession for up to 15 years.
- 23% (5) of study participants have been in the hospitality profession for more than 20 years.

Years in present position:
- 36% (8) of study participants have been in their present position up to 3 years.
- 32% (7) of study participants have been in their present position 3 to 5 years.
- 32% (7) of study participants have been in their present position 5 years or more.

Age:
- 54% (12) of study participants are 30 to 50 years old.
- 23% (5) of study participants are more than 50 years old.
- 23% (5) of study participants are up to 30 years old.
- Gender:
- 68% (15) of study participants are male.
- 32% (7) of study participants are female.
- Area of the country where working:
- 32% (7) of study participants work in the North.
- 23% (5) of study participants work in the West.
- 23% (5) of study participants work in the South.
- 14% (3) of study participants work in the Mountain region of the country.
- 9% (2) of study participants work in the Central region of the country.

Amount of management functions performed:
- 55% (12) of study participants state that they perform many (> 7).
- 36% (8) of study participants state that they perform a moderate amount (4-6).
- 9% (2) of study participants state they perform few (1-3).

Number of direct reports:
- 55% (12) of study participants supervise seven or more direct reports.
- 36%(8) of study participants supervise 4 to 6 direct reports.
- 9% (2) of study participants supervise 1 to 3 direct reports.

Those using goal setting daily:

- 95% (21) of study participants use principles of goal setting daily.
- 5% (1) of study participants do not use principles of goal setting daily.

Does goal setting increase your organization's bottom line?

- 76% (16) of study participants say goal setting increases their bottom line by 15% or more.
- 24% (5) of study participants say goal setting increases their bottom line 10 up to 15%.
- 0% (0) of study participants say goal setting increases their bottom line less than 10%.

Benefits of goal setting:

Interview participants mentioned a variety of benefits that are derived from goal setting. Through focus questions, I was able to categorize their answers into four major categories including:

- Directing attention.
- Encouraging high-level performance.
- Developing innovation and persistence.
- Reducing stress.

Steps of goal setting:

Interview participants mentioned a variety of steps they use in the goal setting process. Through focus questions, I was able to categorize their answers into six major steps including:

- Specifying the goal and how to accomplish it.
- Creating a SMART goal—specific, measurable, acceptable, realistic, and timely.
- Identifying resource sources and evaluating risk involved.
- Obtaining feedback.

Approaches to goal achieving:

Interview participants mentioned two approaches that they utilize for achieving goals:

- Visualization.
- Setting objectives.

Coaching methods:

Interview participants mentioned a variety of methods they utilize in effectively coaching their employees toward goal achievement. Through focus questions, I was able to categorize their answers into 10 categories including:

- Staying in contact.
- Praising employees.
- Communicating the importance of the process.
- Ensuring employee capability.
- Allowing employees to reward and review themselves.
- Choosing the right time.
- Choosing the right motivational methods.
- Publicizing goals.
- Using negative feedback.
- Avoiding goal conflict.

Implications and Lessons

Findings help support my hunches. However, with the small sample (n=22), I cannot generalize findings to the larger population of hospitality managers.

The panel of participants indicates an increase in the business pace due to competition, smaller staffs due to reorganization, and higher expectations by their ownership. The majority of respondents (68 percent) have been in their present jobs five years or less—a shorter time than I expected. While some of the job turnover can be accounted for by advancement, much of the turnover is due to turmoil. Fortunately, managers' skills are portable; as 87 percent of study participants have been in the hospitality industry at least 10 years.

Findings indicate that it is still a "man's world" in the higher ranks of the hospitality industry within the sample population. Men outnumber women by more than two to one as managers.

Participants describe their management functions as "many" (7 or more) indicating that these truly are managers in the sense that they exercise a broad spectrum of general management responsibilities in the areas of planning, organizing, coordinating, and controlling, as opposed to the narrow focus of technical segment specialists. This may help explain the seemingly large number of direct reports managers supervise.

It is in the coordinating function that I am a bit surprised—specifically span of control (the number of people who report to one manager). The majority of manager participants (55 percent) supervise at least seven employees. While I classified the highest category as seven or more; the average within this category is 10. One manager supervises 15. Managers indicate their having a wider span of control necessitates a system such as goal setting to help organize the interaction and communication among their employees.

The fact that 95 percent of the study participants utilize the principles of goal setting on a daily basis is as I expected. I am puzzled to find that one manager—considered by most measures as quite successful—does not use goal setting. This finding may provide the basis for an interesting future study.

The finding that 76 percent of participants believe that goal setting has a positive effect on their organizations' bottom lines by at least 15 percent is particularly noteworthy. When I set out to undertake this study I thought that managers would say that the outcome is worth the time and effort. However, I did not anticipate such dramatic results. An unexpectedly large 19 percent of study participants say that goal setting improves their bottom lines by over 20 percent.

Finally, I was interested to hear managers' thoughts concerning the goal-setting process as a whole. Relating back to their comments about their work being more demanding than in the past, manager participants believe that they must first be able to manage themselves before they can manage others. In other words, managers must implement an effective system of goal setting and achieving for themselves before they can embark upon an organization-wide goal setting program for others.

Future Ideas
Seizing Opportunity

I was intrigued to find one successful manager, a chief operating officer that does not use goal-setting methods per se. His techniques include focusing on opportunities that arise. Here are some excerpts from my write up: "I believe that when my chance happens I must focus on that opportunity or it will come and go without positive results. I wanted to do well in my career…but I never got too specific."

While the majority (21 of 22 participants) of the managers in this study clearly utilize goal-setting methods on a regular basis, it may be interesting to examine the balance between focusing on goals and seizing unexpected opportunities as they arise.

Benefits

Study participants believe goals help managers translate general intentions into specific actions. Debra Mesch defines a goal as a plan for a desired outcome.[23] And goal-setting theory posits that people who set goals perform more effectively than those who do not set goals.[24] David Chag, GM of the Country Club of Brookline, Massachusetts, states, "Goals establish an end result, a direction of pursuit, a method of measurement, and foster team work and achievement. Goals help us perform beyond our capabilities and keep us focused when the going gets tough."

There are many benefits of goal setting. Some of the more notable advantages identified by study participants include:

- Directing attention and actions because they give managers a target.[25] People can become confused if they do not have a specific goal toward which to direct their efforts. Goals nurture an atmosphere that produces specific results within specific time periods.
- Performing at peak levels. Setting goals makes managers aware of the mental, emotional, and physical energy they will need for the task and encourages them to conserve and mobilize energy carefully.
- Bolstering persistence. The absence of strong goals can distract from one's mission and foster a temptation to quit when facing a challenge.
- Developing innovative strategies. Managers that set important goals will be surprised at how ingenious they can be in devising their strategies to reach their goals.

- Providing a short and long-term game plan. If set properly and realistically, managers can map out their futures with their companies, or effect plans to achieve other aspirations.
- Preventing stress. A comprehensive goals program can help avoid burnout and produce positive feelings.[26]

Steps in Establishing a Goal
Step One: Identify the Problem

As a first step toward goal setting, specify exactly what is to be accomplished: the job, assignment, or responsibility. Managers can use brainstorming methods to assist in identifying problems and then rank the ideas that emerge.

Brainstorming

Create a list of wants or desires as they relate to the job, assignment, or responsibility. Try to put aside inhibitions and be creative—in a dreamlike state. This is the time to catalog all options. Resist the temptation to evaluate whether or not these dreams are practical, logical, or even possible. Jerry McCoy, a certified club manager and consultant living in Columbus, Georgia, shared these thoughts about the brainstorming process: "Our most successful and creative ideas come from brainstorming. We brainstorm for special projects and in general sessions to help improve overall operations."

Ranking

Next, prioritize to determine which of these desires is most important. Select the most important option as the goal.

Step Two: Map Strategy

Create a plan for how to accomplish the goal. Brainstorm to develop a list of possible alternatives—regardless of how impractical they appear. After recording possibilities, begin the culling process by considering the limitations of each alternative. Discard those that are unreasonable.

Step Three: Set a SMART Performance Goal

A SMART goal is a goal that is: Specific, measurable, acceptable, realistic, and timely. The following points discuss the importance of incorporating these five components into the goal-setting process.

Specific

Goals should be both explicit and unclouded—something to aim toward without misinterpretation. It is not enough simply to set positive-sounding goals ("I want to become more fit"). O'Hair found managers are more likely to succeed if their goals are specific and clear.[27] Harry Waddington, GM of the Piedmont Driving Club in Atlanta believes, "Focus is the key to my success. If I focus specifically on something long enough, I know that I probably can achieve it. If we properly plan a function and carefully focus on the details as it unfolds, we are likely to produce a huge success."

Goal-setting theory asserts that specific goals improve performance by producing higher levels of effort and planning than unclear or general goals. People strive for a higher standard of success by increasing effort.[28] When people pursue vague goals, they may obtain satisfaction from even low levels of performance.[29]

Managers can channel some of this extra effort into the development of appropriate plans. Studies show that people with specific goals tend to plan and organize more than those with general goals that, in turn, create a motivational effect to follow through with the plan.[30] Using the example about desiring to become more physically fit begins to transform from a general wish to a distinct possibility by amending the statement to the more specific statement, "I will become more physically fit by beginning a jogging program." This idea becomes more salient and develops into a goal as the process evolves.

Measurable

It is very important that goals are measurable because measurement permits objectivity that helps define goals in terms of actions that one can readily see. Measurement can be as simple as an informal check list, or it may be a complex and sophisticated evaluation form that measures performance in a variety of categories. For example, at the beginning of your jogging program, you could establish a baseline by timing yourself over a one-mile course. If your time is 14 minutes, you have established that as your baseline. It is reasonable to infer that with proper training, your time can improve—an indication of enhanced fitness. You may decide that you will jog 45 minutes, five days a week, for four weeks. And at the beginning of each week, you will time your first mile to see how you are progressing.

Acceptable

Goals should not be imposed, but rather self-desired and thereby acceptable—whether assigned or self conceived. When managers accept their goals and make a commitment to achieving them, goals have a much better chance of being realized. However, if the goal is more imposed than desired, the goal may be perceived as more difficult to attain, thereby resulting in frustration instead of accomplishment. Is achieving an improved fitness level an acceptable, self-desired goal to you—one that you are committed to achieving?

Acceptance and commitment create determination for reaching a goal—regardless of the goal's origin. Locke summarized the determinants of goal acceptance and commitment into three categories: external influences, interactive factors, and internal factors.[31]

External influences—legitimate authority. Managers have both personal and work related goals. Companies have goals that are often times pushed down on managers from higher levels such as from corporate, to division, to region, and to the property level. In order for managers to be as effective as possible in goal achievement, they must deal with this dilemma of sorting out which goals are most important. In effect, managers must try to reconcile conflicting goals and attempt to make them congruent for themselves as well as for those they supervise. This merging of individual and organizational needs is seen as the biggest challenge in goal attainment.[32]

Managers should take responsibility for and assume ownership of their goals—all goals. Those that are sent down from the corporate or divisional offices should be carefully incorporated as guiding principles into property-level goals where they become more salient. It may not be easy. The culture of the organization will regulate the amount of influence managers have on top-down goals. Michael Mooney, manager at the Annapolis Yacht Club in Maryland offered insight regarding his past experience in a restaurant company: "Corporate set the goals, the general managers were the enforcers. Department heads had very little say. Now that I am a manager, I try to involve everyone in the process, so our goals become more meaningful."

Ideally, managers should go about the process of developing and implementing work-related goals with the same structure and zeal they would utilize with their personal goals, instead of accepting them as habitual responses, respect for authority, or due to the power of the person assigning the goal.[33] With long work weeks the norm for hospitality managers, the process of buying off on and personalizing organizational goals is a key issue with which to make peace.

Assigned goals do the following:[34]

- Afford a feeling of purpose, guidance, and explicitness concerning expectations.
- Broaden individuals' convictions of what they think they can realize.
- 3. Direct individuals toward developing high quality plans to realize their goals.
- Interactive factors—participation and competition. Although assigned goals increase commitment, studies suggest that participatory goal setting produces even greater commitment. Participation was a subject of primary concern to management during the 1960s.[35] Maier's research asserts that employees tend to set higher goals for themselves in a participatory setting than supervisors alone would dare to impose, since employees seem to be more acutely aware of the factors within their control.[36]

Studies have not yet definitively proven how competition affects commitment. However, Locke found that employees set significantly higher goals and performed significantly better in competitive situations than those who were not competing.[37]

Internal factors—personal goals, self efficacy and internal rewards. Personal goals and self efficacy judgments have direct effects on performance. Zander suggested that individuals are equally committed to self-set and participatively-set goals.[38]

Individuals will set more difficult personal goals for themselves than for others because they see themselves as more able to perform. In other words, individuals have lower expectations for others than for themselves. "We see evidence of this all the time. Our corporate targets are quite aggressive, but our managers set even higher goals for themselves. Essentially, they become entrepreneurs within a billion dollar organization," states Ed Evans, vice president of human resources for the Business Services Group of ARAMARK.

During the goal-setting process, individuals experience a normative shift that shapes their self-efficacy—the belief in their capabilities.[39] When an individual believes that they can accomplish a task, they will push themselves. By contrast, not even incentives will motivate an individual with low self-efficacy. In other words, self-efficacy is more a more fundamental internal value than reward. People will not strive for rewards they believe are unattainable, but they will commit to goals they believe they can reach.

Realistic

Not only should goals be specific, they should also be challenging—but within an individual's capabilities and limitations. Goals should not represent whatever levels of achievement a manager decides would be "nice." Dreaming has no place in effective goal setting. For goals to serve as a tool for stretching an individual to reach their full potential, they must be challenging but achievable. Therefore, before beginning goal setting, managers should consider their stretch capabilities and honestly examine whether they have the knowledge, skills, resources, and abilities needed in successfully accomplishing their goals. Satisfying this criterion means setting goals in light of several important considerations:[40]

- What performance levels will conditions realistically allow?
- What results will it take to be a successful performer?
- What is an individual capable of accomplishing when pushed?

Managers should emphasize that their goals extend their abilities. Though it may take extra determination and hard work to achieve difficult goals, it will be far more rewarding than those goals that can be achieved with little effort. Research has found that when challenging goals are set instead of easy goals, performance is usually better. This is true because achieving only easy goals may keep one from realizing their full potential.[41] Bill Kendall of Woodmont Country Club in Rockville, Maryland states, "The process of lofty goal setting keeps everyone striving for improvement, rather than allowing the easier alternative. We want our managers continually stretching their limits." On the other hand, managers should not set goals that will be impossible to achieve, thereby setting themselves up for failure. Experiencing failure makes people less apt to set goals in the future.

For example, you probably will never be able to run a four-minute mile, so stating that as a goal for your fitness program is not productive. But it is a good idea to push yourself beyond what you honestly feel would be your best performance. You know from your baseline measurement that you can jog a 14-minute mile in your present fitness condition. Furthermore, you may remember three years ago, after one month of easy-to-moderate training, you were able to run a 12-minute mile. To set that as a goal would not allow you to reach your full potential. On the other hand, you may feel that if you really train hard, you may be able to jog a 10-minute mile—two minutes faster than ever before. The 10-minute mile goal—one that broadens your previous capability—will be a far more rewarding goal.

Timely

Managers should not constrain themselves with procedures and deadlines. While goals should be specific, they must be allowed to change over time. "As the world evolves, circumstances change," says Mohammad Memar'Sadeghi, manager at the Carousel Hotel, Resort, and Athletic Club in Ocean City, Maryland. "We can't just set and achieve goals in a vacuum—there are too many external variables such as weather, regulations, or economics affecting our business. We must be able to change too—even if it means abandoning a goal altogether and creating a new one." Setting highly specific, inflexible goals may give a manager an unfavorable reputation as being too rigid, or unresponsive to the real world. For example, if you have set achievement of your 10-minute mile goal over a four-week timeline and sprain your ankle at the end of the third week, you will likely need to adjust your deadline.

Step Four: Identify Necessary Resources

Time, equipment, money, favors, encouragement, and moral support are just a few of the resources managers may need to achieve their goals. Anticipating resource needs will strengthen plans and actions, and planning how to utilize resources can make goals more real and concrete. Using the 10-minute mile example, you should consider issues such as how you will work your run into your daily schedule, where you will keep your workout clothes (and your new $135 Nikes), how you will freshen-up afterward, and if your staff will support your quest— after all, they are bound to enjoy the stress-relieving benefits that come from your fitness program!

Step Five: Recognize Risk, Contingencies, and Conflict

Risk

To increase the probability of success, consider the risks connected with accomplishing the goal. Risks refer to what might be lost by pursuing the goal by one method over other alternatives identified in the brainstorming process. In your 10-minute mile quest, how much higher is your risk of injury (and perhaps goal failure) if you use your old Nikes instead of spending $135 for a new pair?

Contingencies

Prepare for contingencies. Do you have an alternate location to run if you live in an area where severe weather is a possibility? Should you consider the possibility of a fitness club membership for showering and changing? What happens if a last-minute meeting comes up as you are walking out of the door to go run? Devise goals so that a large number of potential obstacles can be removed or mitigated in order to have a better shot at achieving the desired end results.

Conflict

When pursuing multiple goals managers will likely devote more time and effort to one goal than another, often trading off between quantity and quality goals. Task difficulty and interest will determine the goal selection and performance. If managers choose difficult quality and quantity goals or if they are not confident of their abilities, they can often feel overloaded and unable to improve. As a result, they will begin to tradeoff performance quality for performance quantity.[42]

One manager expressed this concept succinctly: "We name proprietary brands in our specifications to make sure our dining patrons are getting the highest quality. Last week we could not buy Ore Ida or Lamb's shoestring fries—just the distributor's private label. Instead of our normal five-ounce portion, we served eight-ounce portions to try to head off any possible complaints."

Step Six: Obtain Feedback

Feedback clarifies messages and verifies shared meaning. Feedback makes goal setting more effective because it indicates when and where managers may need to adjust their direction or methods so that they are achieving their best.

Feedback can also provide encouragement. If managers receive messages that support their goals and their progress toward them, they are more likely to reach those goals and set higher ones in the future.[43]

Goal-setting theory states that feedback results in higher effort and performance than lack of feedback.[44] People use feedback to compare the difference between their performance and established goals and make necessary adjustments. When an individual receives negative feedback, he or she feels dissatisfied because their performance does not meet established standards. Individuals respond to negative feedback by setting higher goals than those that receive positive feedback. The dissatisfaction from negative feedback prompts them to develop more task strategies than those that received positive feedback.[45]

In the short term, negative feedback positively affects goal setting. However, at a certain point the dissatisfaction created by negative feedback can outweigh the benefits. High levels of dissatisfaction can lead to negative behavior and an increase in absenteeism and employee turnover. Even in the short term, negative feedback can be detrimental if the individual does not believe his effort ever will result in positive feedback. Negative feedback might not be appropriate when there is a lack of organizational support, low trust, a poor relationship with the feedback source, and low self efficacy. Conversely, a positive relationship with the feedback source, a high-trust environment, support for goal accomplishment, high self efficacy, and rigorous criteria for acceptable performance may enhance the feedback relationship.[46]

Furthermore, the more difficult and more specific goals become, the more feedback managers need. In essence, the process reinforces itself: Setting higher goals leads to better effort and elevated performance; learning of success through feedback encourages still higher goals in the future.[47] Talk about your 10-minute mile goal with other runners, read running magazines, try an organized fun run event. Develop an informal support group that can provide constructive feedback regarding your goal.

Goal selection and establishment using the preceding steps are perhaps the most important stages in establishing what people want to do. By this time in the process:

- The goal should be identified.
- A strategy for how the goal will be accomplished should be mapped out.
- The performance goal should be challenging, flexible, and measurable.
- Issues such as time, money, and other necessary resources for goal achievement should have been considered.
- Risk and rewards relative to the alternative selected should be understood. Similarly, a well-devised strategy for contingencies that may arise should be in place.
- Finally, a support group for receiving constructive feedback from others should be assembled.

Create a Written Goal Statement

When the decisions in the steps for establishing a goal have been successfully made, commit them to writing. Review and adjust or clarify the steps as necessary. Be specific. Using the information produced in the step process, create a written goal statement that includes answers to the following points:

Who? Sam Jones.

What? Adopt the goal to run a 10-minute mile.

Where? On the track at Canyon College.

When? Within four weeks of beginning my jogging program January 1. (Without a deadline, there is less urgency, resulting in laxness and the risk of losing interest.)

Why? I have selected this goal to help me begin a jogging program.

How? I will schedule my 45-minute jogging routine five days per week—just like any other appointment.

Who cares? A regular jogging program will enable me to become physically fit, reduce stress, and allow me uninterrupted time to think about the strategic direction of my resort.

Once written, the goal will have more meaning and importance to the creator. Beverly Schlegel, manager of the

Shenandoah Club in Roanoke, Virginia adds, "I first became familiar with the importance of the goal-setting process in high school. Our journalism teacher pounded it into our heads at every opportunity. To this day, I still ask those questions, not only when I write, but when I plan. This format is a major key to our success." Once the goal is established, move forward to the physical and cognitive steps of goal setting.

Achieving the Goal

Before beginning the achievement phase of the goal there should now exist an established, written goal. The written goal statement is a declaration of the outcome one plans to accomplish. Now consider how and when to accomplish the goal. Two of the effective ways to approach the achievement of one's goals are the cognitive approach and the physical approach.

The Cognitive Approach—Visualization

The cognitive approach takes place within the mind. It is a mental procedure, a visualization. The fundamental premise behind visualization assumes that the subconscious cannot distinguish between an actual experience and one vividly imagined. By concentrating on the goal and believing that it is attainable, it is likely that the subconscious mind will begin to play a role in helping with goal achievement. Sherrie Laveroni, regional vice president and managing director of the Regency Hotel in New York City, confirms the value of the visualization process: "When you set a goal, you set into motion 'possibility.' Possibility for something better, greater. You immediately are activated to plan and imagine what could be . . . and how to make it happen."

There are four steps involved with visualization that will prove beneficial toward the final outcome:

- Develop an enthusiastic and positive attitude. Have confidence that the goal is attainable. If not, no amount of work will be able to overcome that fault.

- Relax. Sit back in a comfortable chair and allow your body to unwind. Close your eyes and breathe easily, slowly, and deeply.
- Imagine accomplishment. Envision success in detail. Fill your mind with thoughts of achievement. Dwell on these positive thoughts and enjoy the pleasant feeling. Now, imagine a single situation where you achieve your goal. Visualize this success repeatedly. Convince yourself that the scenario exists. Repetition is important in helping convince the subconscious that the success is real.
- Reorientation. After an intense session, clear your mind. Allow time to reorient with your surroundings and resume your daily activities. This may be helpful in avoiding any possible obsession or loss of touch with reality regarding the goal.

Physical Approach—Setting Objectives

The physical approach is the doing as opposed to the thinking orientation of the cognitive approach. The physical approach includes the setting of objectives. Objectives are short-term milestones that enable managers to map out the conditions that must be met for goals to be reached.[48] Lou Krouse, chairman of the board of Stein Eriksen Lodge, in Deer Valley, Utah, shares his opinion of the importance of setting objectives: "With the Olympic Games in our back yard, our senior management team is ferocious about setting and achieving objectives. With hundreds of projects and tasks to finalize before the athletes, tourists, and media descend upon our resort area, end-result goals would just be too complex to accomplish without interim objectives." Just as there are steps to establishing a goal, and visualizing it, there are steps in setting objectives.

Establish the time frame. Set a period for accomplishing the goal. Evaluate how time is spent, eliminating or spending less time on minor activities to allow more time for goal-achieving activities.

Set interim goals. Break goals into a series of small stepping-stones that will lead to accomplishment of the main goal. Interim successes will help reinforce these steps and inspire you to press onward. The goal becomes more manageable and less overwhelming when goals are broken down into objectives.

Set a deadline. Regular deadlines act as powerful motivators in helping managers reach their goals. Deadlines help determine what must be accomplished and how it must be accomplished. Be as specific as possible. Set periodic checks to determine closeness to achieving the goal and reassess progress. Determine where expectations have been met, exceeded, or fallen short of the goal. If deficient, take appropriate action to get back on schedule.

Recording Progress

An important facet of goal achieving is keeping accurate records of the progress made toward goal accomplishment. Progress will likely come as slow transformation that is not readily recognized without accurate recording of daily activities. It is important, therefore, to maintain precise records. There are two basic methods for recording behavior:

Frequency Count

A frequency count involves calculating the number of times a particular event occurs. This is perhaps the easiest and most common method of assessment. For example, if you have committed to jogging five times per week in your 10-minute mile goal, a frequency count will help assess progress being made.

Time Duration

This method involves timing the length of the activity. If you have committed to jogging for 45 minutes each session in your 10-minute mile goal, you can keep track of your progress by using the chronograph feature of a sports watch.

Reinforcing

Knowing how to measure the progress of goal accomplishment, one should also establish appropriate methods for reward and discipline when accomplishing or falling short on making progress toward the goal.

In choosing to use positive (reward) and negative (discipline) reinforcers, ensure that the criteria are realistic and attainable. By establishing criteria, managers have measurable control as to what degree a reward or discipline will be administered.

It is important to experience small rewards such as positive self acknowledgment early and frequently to help increase the likelihood of maintaining the goal quest. Similarly, discipline for non achievement should not be so severe as to cause one to give up.

Small lapses and regressions may occur during the process. Do not permit them to cause discouragement. Rather, let the lapse become the impetus for renewed and redoubled effort toward the goal.

Goal Aids

Aids are utilized to help managers keep their goals before them at all times—ever-present but not intrusive. They are most effective when practiced on a daily basis.

One club executive uses time spent in driving to work as quiet time for reviewing and emphasizing goal aspiration. A hotel general manager does daily step exercises to the accompaniment of "I wish to be a regional vice president, I want to be a regional vice president, I will be a regional vice president"—from fantasy, to desire, to determination.

Goal Re-evaluation

Goals are likely to change with time. There is nothing wrong with that. However, the decision to change goals should be both rational and conscious. Where accomplishment was underestimated, set higher goals. Similarly, where accomplishment was overestimated, this is the time to adjust to more realistic goals (just be sure to keep them challenging). Re-evaluate. Have efforts been maximized? Was the goal attainable and realistic within the established time period? Re-evaluation means re-thinking and making necessary adjustments. It does not mean quitting.

Re-evaluation may indicate the desirability of changing an interim goal. Do so, if necessary. The aim is to achieve the goal, not to let it beat you. Tom Hale, CEO of Myrtle Beach National, a resort company in South Carolina, offered his view on the re-evaluation process: "We have to constantly re-think our interim goals and objectives. If we see that our guests' preferences are changing, we must determine how to best meet those needs—now and in the future. Often that means altering our goals and objectives to provide the level of service desired."

Techniques for use in Managing Others Through Goal Setting

Once managers have established their goals, and have moved toward achieving them successfully, they can begin to coach their employees on goal setting. Bob Sexton, Certified Hospitality Educator and consultant from Rancho Mirage, California, had this to say: "Goal setting cannot be implemented without effective, regular coaching. I ensure that goals:
- Are created by those that will achieve them
- Have measurable mileposts along the way
- Include incentive
- Build in steps from simple to difficult
- Are split between objective and subjective measures."

Employees should choose and set goals for themselves using the same methods that have been described above. Managers should encourage employees to set both personal goals and those that relate to their work performance. Norm Spitzig, GM at BallenIsles Country Club in Palm Beach Gardens, Florida describes his process: "I spend a good deal of time with each member of my senior management team asking them to come up with seven to ten major goals they want to accomplish. I also have my own list—again seven to ten in number. We discuss all of the goals, eliminate those that are unrealistic or un-measurable, modify others, and adopt some as they are. We eventually agree on the specific goals."

Managers may want to share one of their job goals as an example to help their employees understand the concept. If managers can institute a program whereby all employees set and achieve goals, their properties will run more efficiently and more productively as the staff will understand where they are going and why they are going there. John Jordan, GM of Cherokee Town and Country Club in Atlanta had this to say: "I meet with my direct reports every week in order to give each individual an hour of my undivided attention without interruption. We use forms as guides to ensure we cover all areas—accomplishments, work in progress, questions, opportunities, work ahead, and comments on the support managers need from me. We even set daily objectives to help achieve goals. I believe that for goals to be achieved successfully, they should be set democratically but implemented dictatorially by the team leader."

Stay in close contact. After employees have begun to establish work goals, managers should review their plans to ensure they are consistent with the larger-perspective organizational goals. Managers should encourage and support their employees' goal-setting efforts. Meet with them on a regular basis to discuss progress, problems, and goal refinement.

Praise often. Words of praise go a long way with many people. If employees are not making progress, discuss reasons why, and if necessary change the goal.

Communicate the importance of the process. If certain employees are not interested in the goal-setting process, managers should explain that it is important to the property and to those employees' growth within the organization. Make sure that employees understand the importance and benefits of goal setting in all aspects of their life. Rick Thorn, manager of San Luis Obispo Golf Club in California, offers his thoughts, "I try to have goals set at the lowest levels of the organization—almost everyone is involved. Once goals are adopted, I meet with my staff on a regular basis to assess how we are progressing and use them as a basis for rating supervisors' performance. Everyone understands the importance of the process."

Make sure employees are capable. Pay close attention to changes in employees' feelings of self-efficacy, recognizing that they are more likely to experience low self confidence in stressful situations, where anxiety replaces motivation. Participatory goal setting can channel anxiety into motivation and increase self-efficacy, leading to greater goal commitment than possible through assigned goals.[49] Managers can raise employee confidence and reduce anxiety by providing information and training and supportive behavior.50

Allow employees to reward and review themselves during the coaching process. Managers can increase organizational commitment and performance by encouraging employees to engage in self-generated rewards and feedback during review sessions. People are more likely to accept and derive meaning from self-generated feedback than from supervisor-generated feedback.[51] Bill Koegler, director of development and planning for Oglebay Resort and Conference Center in Wheeling, West Virginia, recalled an example from his general manager days at the resort: "We'd established a creative plan to increase occupancy, but realized that the front desk wasn't pushing the plan in order to avoid the possible embarrassment associated with overbooking. We asked them to come up with a plan. They created a reward system that divided the revenue from the last room rented among the staff. Instead of six to seven empty rooms, we got down to averaging one or two."

Choose the right time. Goals may be presented at the beginning of a week, a new project, or when quarterly reports or performance appraisals are given. If there is a time lag between the assignment of a goal and performance, additional information input that intervenes in the process may cause changes in the originally set goals and distract attention necessary to reach the desired performance level.[52]

Select the right method. During the early stages of skill acquisition, performance goals may be distracting and, therefore, counterproductive. Different types of goals (e.g., learning vs. performance) may be helpful during different phases of skill acquisition.[53] For example, if you wish to increase productivity in the engineering department, then you should assign a difficult performance goal rather than a do-your-best job, or no productivity goal.

Publicize goals. Managers can increase goal commitment to goals by making goals public rather than keeping them private. The public spotlight and pressure will help motivate commitment.

Consider using negative feedback. Managers who expect more from their subordinates often achieve better performance than those who demand less. If trust and a good relationship are present, negative feedback can help increase and motivate employee performance. But, this word of caution: If managers plan to give negative feedback, they should be sure to give it in a specific, non-evaluative way so that employees are challenged to work harder to achieve.[54]

Avoid goal conflict. Managers should ensure that individual goals facilitate the attainment of organizational goals.[55] If managers reward employees for a quantity goal while being asked to make a quality goal a top priority, they will commit less to both the quantity and quality goals.[56]

Summary

Managers are expected to perform a multitude of functions including planning, organizing, leading, and controlling, and perhaps most important, executing their responsibilities through others. Managers cannot expect to manage others if they cannot manage themselves. Establishing a system of goals is a valuable tool that will enable managers to do both—manage themselves and others.

Managers should recognize some of the many benefits of goal setting including:
- Directing attention and actions.
- Mobilizing peak-level performance.
- Bolstering persistence.
- Developing innovative strategies.
- Providing a short and long-term game plan.
- Preventing stress and burnout.

As a first step toward goal setting, identify the problem. Specify what is to be accomplished: the job, assignment, or responsibility to be completed. Managers can use brainstorming methods to assist in identifying problems and then rank the ideas that emerge.

The second step includes creating a plan for how to accomplish the goal. Develop a list of all possible alternatives and then discard those that are unreasonable.

Step three lists elements to include when creating a SMART performance goal. SMART goals are those that are: specific, measurable, attainable, realistic, and timely.

Step four identifies resources such as time, equipment, money, favors, encouragement, and moral support managers may need to achieve their goals. Anticipating resource needs will strengthen plans and actions, and planning how to utilize resources can make goals more real and concrete.

Step five refers to the risk involved by pursuing the goal using one method over another, planning for potential obstacles that develop, and the eventual trade offs among conflicting goals. Trading off between quantity and quality goals is one of the most common conflicts.

Step six discusses the need for constructive feedback. Feedback makes goal setting effective because it indicates when and where managers may need to adjust their direction or methods so that they are achieving their best.

When the decisions in the steps for establishing a goal have been successfully made, commit them to writing. The goal statement is a declaration of the outcome one plans to accomplish. Review and adjust or clarify the steps as necessary. Be specific. Using the information produced in the step process, create a written goal statement that provides the answers to who, what, when, where, why, how, and who cares?

Once an established, written goal exists, managers can then move toward achievement of the goal. Two of the effective ways to approach goal achievement are the cognitive approach and the physical approach. The cognitive approach is a mental procedure, a visualization that assumes that by concentrating on the goal and believing that it is attainable, it is likely that the subconscious mind will begin to play a valuable role in helping with goal achievement.

The physical approach includes the setting of objectives that enable managers to reach their goals. Just as there are steps to establishing a goal, and visualizing it, there are steps in setting objectives:

State the requirements and methods.

Establish the timeframe.

Set interim goals.

Set a deadline.

An important facet of goal achieving is keeping accurate records of the progress made toward goal accomplishment. The fact that progress will likely come as slow transformation makes it important to keep precise records by frequency count or time duration.

Managers should also establish appropriate methods for reward and discipline when accomplishing or falling short on making progress toward the goal. Positive (reward) and negative (discipline) reinforcers, ensure that the criteria are realistic and attainable. It is important to experience small rewards early and frequently to help increase the likelihood of maintaining the goal quest. Similarly, small lapses and regressions may occur during the process. Discipline for non achievement should not be so severe as to cause one to give up.

Goal aids are utilized to help managers keep their goals before them at all times—ever-present but not intrusive. They are most effective when practiced on a daily basis such as during the morning commute or during exercise periods.

Goals are likely to change with time and therefore should be re-evaluated. However, the decision to change goals should be both rational and conscious. Where accomplishment was underestimated, set higher goals. Similarly, where accomplishment was overestimated, this is the time to adjust to more realistic goals.

Once managers have established their goals, and have moved toward achieving them successfully, they can begin to coach their employees on goal setting. These are some effective methods managers can use in coaching their employees:

Stay in close contact. Find out what support employees need from you to be successful.

Praise often. Compliments help employees feel appreciated and valuable to the goal achievement process.

Communicate the importance of the process to everyone involved.

Make sure employees are capable of achieving the goal.

Allow employees to reward and review themselves. People are more likely to accept and derive meaning from self-generated feedback than from supervisor-generated feedback.

Choose the right time. A time lag between the assignment and actual achieving of the goal may cause changes in the originally set goals and thereby distract attention away from the goal.

Select the right method. Different types of goals such as learning goals may be helpful and more appropriate to set than performance goals when people are acquiring information and skills.

Publicize goals. The public spotlight and pressure will help motivate commitment.

Consider using negative feedback. But, this word of caution: If managers plan to give negative feedback, they should be sure to give it in a specific, non-evaluative way so that employees are challenged to work harder to achieve.

Avoid goal conflict. Managers must ensure that individual goals facilitate (rather than conflict with) the attainment of organizational goals.

Summary of classifications: 2 Owners, 3 Corporate Executives, 4 District or Regional Managers, 10 General Managers, and 3 Managers.

Bibliography

Earley, Christopher P, William Prest, and Pauline Wojnaroski. "Task Planning and Energy Expended: Exploration of How Goals Influence Performance." *Journal of Applied Psychology*, Vol.72, No.1, (1987), pp. 107-114.

Gardner, M., *The Annotated Alice: Alice's Adventures in Wonderland & Through the Looking Glass* (New York: Clarkson N. Potter, Inc., 1960), p. 88.

Gatewood, R. D., Taylor, R. R., and Ferrell, O. C., *Management Comprehension, Analysis, and Application.* (Burr Ridge, IL: Richard D. Irwin, Inc., 1995).

Gellatly, Ian R. and John P. Meyer. "The Effects of Goal Difficulty on Physiological Arousal, Cognition, and Task

Performance." *Journal of Applied Psychology*, Vol.77, No.5, (1992), pp. 694-704.

Gilliland, Stephen W. and Ronald S. Lamis. "Quality and Quantity Goals in a Complex Decision Task: Strategies and Outcomes." *Journal of Applied Psychology*, Vol.77, No.5, (1992), pp. 672-681.

Latham, Gary P. and Edwin A. Locke. "Self-Regulation Through Goal Setting." *Organizational Behavior and Human Decision Processes*, 50, (1991), pp. 212-247.

Locke, E. A., Chah, D., Harrison, S., and Lustgarten, N. "Separating the Effects of Goal Specificity From Goal Level." *Organizational Behavior and Human Decision Making*, 43, (1989), pp. 270-287.

Locke, Edwin A. "The Determinants of Goal Commitment." *Academy of Management Review*, Vol.13, No.1, (1988), pp. 23-39.

Locke, E. A. and Latham, G. P. *A Theory of Goal Setting and Task Performance* (Englewood Cliffs, NJ: Prentice Hall, 1990).

Maier, Norman R. F. "Assets and Liabilities in Group Problem Solving: The Need for an Integrative Function." *Psychological Review*, Vol.74(4), (1967), pp.233-249.

Mathis, R. L. and Jackson, J. H. (1997). *Human Resource Management* (St. Paul, MN: West Publishing Co., 1997).

Matthews, Linda M., Terence R. Mitchell, Jane George-Flavy, and Robert E. Wood. "Goal Selection in a Simulated Managerial Environment." *Group and Organization Management*, Vol.19, No.4, (December 1994), pp. 425-449.

Mesch, Debra J., Jiing-Lih Farh, and Philip M. Podsakoff. "Effects of Feedback Signs on Group Goal Setting, Strategies, and Performance." *Group and Organization Management*, Vol.19, No.3, (September 1994), pp. 309-333.

Mitchell, Terence R. and William S. Silver. "Individual and Group Goals When Workers Are Interdependent: Effects on Task Strategies and Performance." *Journal of Applied Psychology*, Vol. 73, No. 2, (1990), pp. 185-193.

O'Hair, D. and Friedrich, G. W. (1992). *Strategic Communication in Business and the Professions* (Boston: Houghton Mifflin Company, 1992).

Shalley, Christina E. "Effects of Productivity Goals, Creativity Goals, and Personal Discretion on Individual Creativity." *Journal of Applied Psychology*, Vol. 76, No.2, (1991), pp. 179-185.

Stallworth, H. (1990, June). "Realistic goals help avoid burnout." *HR Magazine*, Vol. 35, 6, (June 1990), p. 171.

Terpstra, David E. and Elizabeth J. Rozell. "The Relationship of Goal Setting to Organizational Profitability." *Group and Organization Management*. Vol. 19, No. 3, (September 1994), pp. 285-294.

Thompson, Jr., A. A. and Strickland III, A. J., *Strategic Management Concepts and Cases.* (Burr-Ridge, IL: Richard D. Irwin, Inc., 1995).

Zander, Alvin, *The Purposes of Groups and Organizations.* (San Francisco: Jossey-Bass Publishers, 1985).

Article 04 Time Management for Restaurant Managers:

No Time Left for You?

Article authors: Florence Berger and Edward A. Merritt

Introduction

"No time for a gentle rain, no time for my watch and chain, no time for revolving doors, no time for the killing floor, there's no time left for you."

When the Guess Who stormed onto the music scene in the early 1970s declaring, "No Time," did they guess that the "who" for which those words would ring true would be a metaphor to describe the pace faced by today's frenzied restaurant managers as well? Some 73% of the respondents to a recent survey by Day Runner Inc. say they are "insanely" busy.[57] Perhaps like never before, managers need to develop effective time management skills in order to stay afloat amid the surging torrents of information, people, and tasks bombarding them.

Statement of the Problem: Why Time Management?

Time management is putting time to the best possible use. But when one considers time management more deeply, it becomes apparent that it is not time, but themselves, that managers must manage. People like to think they are masters of their own time; in reality, most are slaves to events. But time management tools alone are unlikely to make people fully productive; the key is understanding time, proper planning, and priority setting.[58] Though simple in concept, time management can be very difficult to implement. The subject has been treated extensively in articles and books, but the problem of poor time management still haunts today's manager. Shelly Fireman, patriarch of Café Concepts, creators of some of New York City's most successful dining establishments including: Redeye

Grill, Brooklyn Diner USA, Hosteria Fiorella, Café Fiorello, and Trattoria Dell'Arte, offered his tongue-in-cheek method for effectively managing time: "I have a 27-hour clock that I bought in a bazaar in Istanbul 18 years ago. With the three extra hours, I exercise, contemplate the world around me, and read an additional book." Dom DiMattia, vice president for human resources, at Café Concepts added: "There's really no secret to effective time management skills. Although managers may have 100 other things going, they must stay focused on what's important and take it one step at a time—and not catastrophize or exaggerate in their minds about the amount of work they have. We all know we get the work done."

First we will discuss some of the details of the study—including its purpose, methodology, findings, and implications and lessons learned. Second, we will begin to gain a better understanding of time management by discussing how restaurateurs manage their time, why they are managing their time poorly, and introduce a diagnostic tool for helping managers account for where their time is going. The third and final section is devoted to implementing solutions that can lead to more effective time management. Topics include breaking bad habits, delegating, eliminating interruptions, and dealing with mounding paperwork. If managers need an incentive to read further, remember that an astounding 91 percent of study participants state that time management skills increase their organizations' bottom lines by at least 10 percent.

About the Study
Purpose
Our purpose was to help restaurant managers develop better time management habits.

Methodology
We conducted in-depth interviews with a stratified sample of 74 (n=74) restaurant managers located throughout the country to help us probe further into our subject of time management.

Our assumptions were that restaurant managers consider time management to be an important component in the successful operation of a restaurant (measured in terms of bottom-line profit), that managers regularly employ some type of time management system, and that their time management systems are not very effective. Furthermore, assuming those findings, we would create a diagnostic instrument to help managers pinpoint problem areas and suggest a tool kit for implementing effective changes in present methods.

Participants

This study was conducted among 74 (n=74) managers working at restaurants and restaurant companies across the United States. Typical position titles include Owner, Corporate Executive, District or Regional Manager, General Manager, and Manager. The interviews were conducted by telephone and mail.

Demographic Information

First, we asked the expert panel to tell us about themselves. The demographic and descriptive information component of the study contains six statements to determine answers to such variables as these:

- Job title.
- Length of time in the restaurant profession.
- Length of time in present position.
- Age.
- Gender.
- In which of five areas of the country they live.

Study Questions

Next, we asked the managers to tell us about their work. Participants were asked six questions to help guide the subject matter. However, interview sessions were allowed to develop on their own to uncover areas of importance. From those answers, extemporaneous focus questions were asked where appropriate to help clarify information:

- If, in addition to their primary restaurant management duties, they also have other management responsibilities.

- Number of direct reports managers supervise.
- If they use time management principles.
- If yes, their effect on the company's bottom line.
- To rate the effectiveness of their time management practices. Four categories (poor, fair, good, and excellent) segmented the responses. The parameters of the categories reflect the relative degree of time management restaurateurs practice. The poor category consists of managers' responses indicating no planning or forethought. The fair category includes managers who plan or attempt to plan, but only in a casual way. The good category includes those managers who consistently plan, using a planner and looking forward into upcoming weeks. The excellent category includes those managers who not only use a planner but also prioritize and update their schedules.
- To list any impediments to more effective time management.

Findings of the Study

Job title:
- 49% (36 individuals) of study participants hold the job title of general manager.
- 28% (21) hold a job title such as area manager or regional manager, corporate executive, or owner.
- 23% (17) hold the job title of manager.

Years in restaurant profession:
- 38% (28) have been in the restaurant profession up to 10 years.
- 35% (26) have been in the restaurant profession at least 15 years.
- 27% (20) have been in the restaurant profession 10 to 15 years.

Years in present position:
- 43% (32) have been in their present positions at least 3 years.

- 33% (24) have been in their present positions 1 to 3 years.
- 24% (18) have been in their present positions up to 1 year.

Age:
- 49% (36) are up to 30 years old.
- 27% (20) are 30 to 40 years old.
- 24% (18) are at least 40 years old.

Gender:
- 73% (54) are male.
- 27% (20) are female.

Area of the country where working:
- 24% (18) work in the South.
- 23% (17) work in the North.
- 22% (16) work in the Central region.
- 16% (12) work in the Mountain region.
- 15% (11) work in the West.

Additional management duties:
- 76% (56) do not perform additional management duties.
- 24% (18) do perform additional management duties.

Number of direct reports:
- 64% (47) supervise 7 or more direct reports.
- 28% (21) supervise 4 to 6 direct reports.
- 8% (6) supervise 1 to 3 direct reports.

Those using time management principles daily:
- 93% (69) use principles of goal setting daily.
- 7% (5) do not use principles of goal setting daily.

Of those that use time management principles daily (69 respondents), does time management increase your company's bottom line?
- 35% (24) say time management increases their bottom line by 20% or more.
- 33% (23) say time management increases their bottom line by 15 to 20%.

- 32% (22) say time management increases their bottom line up to 15%.

Effectiveness of time management skills:

- 54% (40) rate the effectiveness of their time management skills as poor.
- 18% (13) rate the effectiveness of their time management skills as fair.
- 16% (12) rate the effectiveness of their time management skills as excellent.
- 12% (9) rate the effectiveness of their time management skills as good.

Reasons for ineffectiveness of time management skills:

Through focus questions, we were able to categorize interview participant answers into four major categories including:

- Interruptions.
- Walk-ins.
- Unnecessary meetings.
- Paperwork.

Implications and Lessons

Findings help support our expectations. While restaurant managers realize the important role that time management plays in business success (as measured by bottom-line effect), they can become sidetracked and succumb to unexpected events of the day. This giving in to urgent incidents produces less than stellar outcomes in terms of time management effectiveness—the majority of our study participants rate poor. However, with our small sample (n=74), we cannot generalize our findings to the larger population of restaurant managers.

Our respondents are relatively new to the restaurant business. More than one third (38 percent) have been in the industry less than 10 years. This finding indicates that, at least in terms of this study, that the opportunity to reach the level of manager comes about rather quickly. On the other hand, we were somewhat surprised to find that only approximately one third (35 percent of our study participants have been in the industry for more than 15 years. Is this a hint that the restaurant business is a young person's industry? Perhaps.

The years in present position suggests lots of turnover. Over one half (57 percent) of our respondents have been in their present jobs three years or less—a shorter time than we expected. While some turnover can be accounted for by advancement and job switching, something is also happening at the other end to create all of the position openings. Growth and expansion likely account for some of the opportunity; however the numbers suggest, too, that managers are leaving the industry.

Almost one half of our study participants are less than 30 years old. Three quarters of our participants are less than 40 years old. These findings suggest that, at least in our study, this is a young person's business.

Where do the others go? If we consider years in the restaurant profession, the turnover, and age of respondents, it suggests that older managers are leaving the business. But why? Is it the frenetic pace? Is it due to lifestyle choices? Is the restaurant business a stepping stone to some other area within the hospitality industry? Are managers leaving the industry altogether? The findings are unclear.

Our findings indicate that it is still a "man's world" in the higher ranks of the hospitality industry within our sample population. Men outnumber women almost three to one as managers.

A significant number of participants—almost one quarter (24 percent)—describe themselves as having other management responsibilities besides their primary duties of restaurant management. We are curious to find such a large percentage of our participants with additional duties. However, these findings are consistent with another study that we have cited within the text of this paper.

The majority of respondents (64 percent) supervise 7 or more direct reports. While this number may be large by other standards of comparison, we are not surprised to find that most of our participants supervise 7 or more direct reports.

The fact that 93 percent of the study participants utilize the principles of time management on a daily basis is as we expected. We find it remarkable that managers credit so much of the importance of time management to their bottom lines (68 percent say time management increases their bottom lines by at least 15 percent); and yet over half (54 percent) of our managers rate poor in their effective use of time management skills.

Toward a Better Understanding
How Restaurateurs Manage Their Time

How do restaurateurs manage their time? Poorly, for the most part. The results of a study by Ferguson and Berger[59] found that, more often than not, restaurateurs felt they lacked the knowledge of adequate time management. Furthermore, Merritt notes in a recent study that when faced with vast amounts of information and forced to make decisions too quickly—and with inadequate knowledge—people can be overcome by stress.[60] We feel lack of knowledge of time management strategies is a major problem affecting the restaurateur as a manager. To navigate successfully the intricacies of management, Lewis suggests time management training to help separate useful information from clutter. According to Monical Pizza Corp. president Harry Bond, with a little scrounging and a willingness to modify lessons from other industries and time-management books, restaurateurs can find a warehouse of educational and training materials for little or no money.[61] Larry Schwartz, owner of daVinci's in Sun Valley, Idaho, believes: "Time management is a matter of constant prioritization: First things first; not easiest things first. At the end of the day, I do a recap and update so important points don't get overlooked."

Why Restaurateurs Manage Their Time Poorly

Why do restaurant managers do so poorly when it comes to time management? Mainly because they do not take the time to anticipate how their days will actually be spent. Throughout the day they become bogged down by interruptions. As stated in the Ferguson/Berger article, "They (restaurant managers) had given up so much control over their time and work space, that they constantly managed in an interrupt mode."62 Heidi Pustovit, general manager of New York City's Café Des Artistes, had this to say about her method of effective management: "I list 'to dos' using a computer—I find it much easier to get it all down and then edit. When I group tasks, all I have to do is copy and paste from the original list."

But are restaurant managers alone? Not really. The day-to-day time-management problem is caused by a set of unexpected events that disturb the planned daily activities and thus change the long-term optimal schedule for managers in all types of industries. Often referred to as "interrupt mode," this type of operating condition includes telephone interruptions, meetings, unexpected visitors, poor delegation, and crises.[63] So the question is, "How can restaurant managers become more effective in managing their time?" Read on for some answers.

Improving Time Management Skills

Improving one's own management of time requires a thorough understanding of time—its nature and demands. A recent study conducted by Food Management[64] revealed that in addition to regular duties, an increasing number of persons describing themselves as "restaurant managers" (21%) are managing other areas these days. In order of frequency, the list of extra responsibilities these managers have taken over include: environmental services, linen services, engineering maintenance, transportation, security and fire services, hotel and volunteer services, mail delivery, unit assistance and pharmacy.

This reality of the restaurant-business atmosphere begs the question, "Just how much can one be expected to do?" Apparently a lot. And, as entrepreneurs, restaurant managers tend to have high energy levels, are high in self-confidence—believing they can handle anything that exists or could conceivably come up, and are typically impatient in matters of passing time.[65] Combining increasing management responsibilities with entrepreneurial characteristics can put a manager on the road to overload and subsequent failure, unless they can find ways to mitigate the problematic conditions. Benjamin Ceasar, manager of the trendy Zuni Café, located in San Francisco, shared this technique for staying ahead: "I continually update lists on small notepads. I find that organizing to-do lists in order of priority and area of the restaurant keeps me on top of the most important issues I am facing." One method to begin to make sense of this phenomenon is to understand more about the nature of time.

- Time exists only in the present instant.
- Time is irreplaceable. We may try to expand the hours in the day by double-booking appointments and compressing schedules, but in the end, such bursts are not sustainable.
- Because time past is gone forever, time can only be managed effectively for the future. Plans must be made now for the effective utilization of impending time.

Analyze Where Time Goes

Time—or lack thereof—is indeed the source of many managers' problems. But the solution is not finding ways to squeeze a few extra hours out of the day. Rather, restaurant executives must change the way they think about time. As recent statistics indicate, the need to escape grueling schedules is more pressing than ever. By killing themselves to accomplish more, restaurateurs are actually being counterproductive, becoming prime targets for heart disease, burnout, depression and just plain unhappiness. Effective executives should analyze where their time actually goes. They should then attempt to manage their time and to cut back unproductive demands on that time. Finally, they should consolidate their discretionary time into the largest possible continuing units of uninterrupted time.[66] "I am relentless about planning the details of my day including scheduling time periods for achieving goals and objectives—even slack, discretionary time to use as make-up time or for projects. I write everything down in my Day-Timer®. But, serving periods are dedicated to our dining guests only—no outside interruptions," states Cheryl Hinkle, general manager of the Bridgetown Grill, Atlanta.

This is the foundation upon which time management rests. From here managers can begin to understand how best to utilize their time. The Ferguson/Berger article outlined what restaurant managers do and how their time is spent. Average restaurant managers spend 35 percent of their time in unscheduled meetings, 17 percent in desk sessions, 13 percent on telephone calls, and 6 percent on touring the operation.[67] While these percentages point out how the time is being allocated; they do not specify the importance of the activities with respect to the manager's goals. This is where managers must do their own research: record in intervals, prioritize, and categorize to determine exactly where the time goes. This process is known as time analysis.

Some of the managers surveyed already used time analysis to a minor extent. They stated that they were currently using a daily planner or a "to do" list. However, this is only the beginning. In an effective time analysis, the manager must record the day's events in 15-minute intervals, prioritize each event, and categorize these into groups such as unscheduled meetings, scheduled meetings, and telephone calls. For practical purposes, the manager can list the categories at the top of a time log and simply record the number of the category in the 15-minute time slot. It is very important to record the function as it happens, rather than at the end of the day or at lunch. This is so because the average manager will tend to forget the quotidian events in the workday.

At the end of the day, managers should refer back to the time log and summarize what was actually accomplished toward achieving their stated goals, and how much time was spent. Although time consuming, this process is necessary to construct a more detailed picture of a manager's day and how effectively time was used to achieve goals.

At the end of the week, the manager should tabulate the amount of time spent on each category and estimate the effectiveness of each day. This will give managers some idea of what consumes their time in a typical workday. Using the analogy of dietary habits, people often find recording what they eat over a set number of days helps expose poor eating habits they might not otherwise have discovered. The same idea is true for keeping a time log. By keeping accurate records of where time actually goes over a specified period of time, managers can discover where their time is not being spent wisely. Without keeping a detailed record, managers may fool themselves into thinking they are effective time managers.

A Restaurant Example: The Starlight Cafe

Before analyzing the time log and its features, we must first acquaint ourselves with The Starlight Cafe and introduce its staff. This medium-sized restaurant is located in a city with minimal seasonal fluctuations. It seats 100 diners in two separate dining rooms, and one private dining room seating an additional 25 patrons. Lunch and dinner are served six days a week; lunch is not served on Saturdays and dinner is not served on Sundays. The bar/lounge doubles as a waiting room. The manager, assistant manager, administrative assistant, and chef all have separate offices. The manager's office is directly behind that of the administrative assistant, while the assistant manager's and chef's offices are near the kitchen.

The restaurant staff includes Pat, the manager; Lee, the assistant manager; Sean, the executive chef; Lisa, the administrative assistant/bookkeeper; twelve full- and part-time cooks and kitchen workers; twenty wait staff working about 30 hours per week each; six hosts; eight bussers; and a bar staff of ten. Each day Pat, the manager arrives at 8:00 AM and usually stays until 6:00 or 7:00 PM. Sean, the executive chef, works from 11:00 AM to 9:00 PM, while Lee the assistant manager arrives at 2:30 PM and works until closing.

At this point Pat has been keeping a time log for one week and is ready to summarize results in the weekly performance and allocation report. A breakdown of the various categories on the log will show managers where their time was spent. Managers must then probe further and analyze how effectively their use of time helped them achieve their desired goals.

Let's begin by investigating the manager's goal performance. We will look at the manager's areas of effectiveness and analyze performance of daily duties, determining which were absolutely necessary and which could have been delegated. The manager should ask, "Did I spend enough time, or too much time, on this or that activity—and was it realistic?"

The manager is shown as ineffective at allocating time toward the things that matter, such as daily goals. Some of these goals were not addressed, while a great deal of time was spent on other matters. The manager must take a hard look at these goals and question if they were necessary at all. Were they important enough to warrant a major portion of the day? The manager might respond that all the goals were important and had to be accomplished for effective control and management. Perhaps, but then Pat should ask whether personal attention was needed to complete these goals. For instance, did Pat have to finish the liquor inventory Thursday, or could it have been completed by someone else? Was it so important and sensitive that it required senior management attention? Does Pat feel the need to complete the employee schedule? Clearly such duties should have been delegated to either the assistant manager or the chef; Pat has wasted valuable time doing work of others. A manager who does not delegate is not managing.

The daily effectiveness chart shows the amount of time spent on each goal. By comparing this to the relative importance or priority of each goal, the manager can decide in each case whether the proper amount of time was spent. Naturally we tend to spend more time on things we enjoy doing and to put off the tasks we do not enjoy. Because of ingrained habits, many managers have difficulty differentiating time spent on the enjoyable versus non-enjoyable goals, since both result in the same feeling of accomplishment. Only a written record will indicate how time is actually being spent; the human memory is too deceiving.

Utilizing the effectiveness chart, a manager will be able to determine which goals are more important, the daily time spent on each, and how much time was needed to complete them. Hiring two prep people, for example, may become a more important task than doing the liquor inventory. But if managers could periodically review their own activities, they could monitor time spent in relation to goal priority and make more informed decisions about those priorities. The manager would be relying less on habits and more on facts.

The manager should review the time log to analyze it for wastes of time, process gaps, and tasks that could have been eliminated, delegated, or reduced. Should Pat be opening the restaurant mail? Is planning out next week's forecast by discussing it at 8:00 AM and 5:00 PM as effective as preparing it between 5:30 and 6:15 PM? Does the value of Pat's time justify watching the technician fix the dish machine?

Ultimately, only the restaurant manager can answer these questions. We can only show managers what to look for and suggest possible changes they could make. By targeting specific areas that need to be reduced, a manager initiates more efficient time management.

An end-of-week analysis can help the manager monitor progress. Segmenting the week into daily percentages, helps provide a weekly average. The manager can then track the week's performance and adjust each week accordingly.

Time logs should continue to be maintained on a random basis. It is human nature to fall back into bad habits and forget such things as conscientious time management.

Implementing Solutions
Improvement

We have now investigated the time log and its analysis. If the manager still feels there is room for improvement, we recommend a three-pronged method designed to facilitate more effective time management:

- Breaking bad time management habits.
- Learning to delegate.
- Eliminating the interrupters.

Breaking Habits

Bad habits? Not me! Few of us recognize our bad habits because we are not consciously aware of them. When a new and better practice is developed, it should be implemented as soon as possible. This reduces the chance of the new practice being lost again to the subconscious mind. The new practice should contrast with the old so as to obviate the need to perform the old. Furthermore, when initiating a new practice, the manager must commit to following through on implementation. An announcement of the change will usually suffice to make the manager duty-bound. And once begun, there should be no excuses for not utilizing the new practice.

Procrastination. The human failing most closely associated with poor time management is that of procrastination. Everyone procrastinates to some extent; there is always something one would rather do than a distasteful task. Procrastination is something to be recognized and faced. You can fight your tendency to procrastinate by following these guidelines:

- Do not try to do it all at once.
- Start anywhere.
- Start imperfectly.
- Start even when you are not in the mood.
- Work no more than 15 minutes at a time.
- Do not duck the most difficult problems.
- Realize that unpleasant tasks do not get easier over time.
- Schedule a "Crazy Day" whereby you work through time-consuming details.
- Take the "drive yourself nuts by doing nothing" approach.[68]

No closure. Another bad habit practiced by managers is not completing a task or a decision the first time. Each time a manager picks up an unfinished task, they must re-familiarize themselves with it again. This not only wastes time but in many instances reduces the quality of the task accomplished or the decision made. The manager's original ideas about the task might not be recalled to assist in the final execution. An effective manager follows through with an initiated task until it is accomplished.

Ineffective communication. Task lists are communicated to the staff in many forms: extemporaneous verbal directions, scribbled notes, and elaborate lists and charts. Effective communication strategies vary in part with the characteristics and conditions of the job at hand. Whatever strategy is most appropriate, a manager should take time to ensure expectations are clear so that the staff will know what is expected of them.

Sweating the small stuff. Some managers are able to face crisis after crisis with complete calm. They make handling difficult situations look simple. However, most managers should negotiate around the small speed bumps that occur during the day, so that there is enough energy left to deal with real crises. One strategy is to determine what causes managers to blow things out of proportion in the first place. Misplaced perfectionism is many times at the root of this problem.

Just say "no." Managers should prioritize their work and distinguish between the important issues that they must handle and the urgent, squeaky-wheel issues that crop up during the day. Often, restaurateurs will over-commit to their bosses, customers, employees, or others, only to find themselves hopelessly behind in their work. When managers cannot say no, they should try compromising. Saying "yes, but not now" may buy the manager the amount of time necessary to work the request in with other tasks and projects and follow-through.

Relying on technology for shortening deadlines. Reynolds[69] warns against the management practice of compressing two weeks' worth of work into one week by relying on available technologies to make the work go quicker. While equipment such as personal computers, cell phones, fax machines, and pagers can increase productivity, the availability of such technology does not translate into a sustainable competitive advantage. The restaurant industry has adjusted its ways of doing business right along with other industries. The timesaving provided by such devices has created a new benchmark. Deadlines are shorter and expectations are higher than ever before.

Plug time leaks. Restaurant managers should be relentless in their quest to manage smarter. And, part of managing smarter is learning the difference between just doing and true managing. True managing includes avoiding over-supervising, avoiding excessive attention to low-yield projects, and working like a craftsperson for more than simply the money.

Delegating

Throughout this discussion we have emphasized the importance of delegation. We will now describe how managers can delegate effectively. Where does this process begin? Analysis of the time log should initiate the first step. Before delegating tasks, managers must identify where their time is being spent and which tasks could be performed by someone else.

Reasons for Delegating:

- Delegation allows more time for thinking and planning.
- The person closest to the activity should be better able to make decisions than a distant superior.
- Delegation tends to encourage initiative of subordinates and to make effective use of their skills. Initiative, in turn, improves morale.
- Delegation tends to reduce decision time, as it eliminates recommendations going toward the superior where the decision is made and subsequent downward communication.
- Delegation develops the skills of subordinates by permitting them to make decisions and apply their knowledge gained from training programs and meetings.

However, the manager must realize that delegation involves the transfer of authority and decision-making, not of actual responsibility. James Ippoliti, owner and general manager of Hooligans Café in Liverpool, New York, had this to say about delegation: "With 85 employees, I have to delegate. We assign department managers by area and empower interested service staff to take on additional duties such as closing and inventory control. While it's a great help to the managers, it also becomes a track by which our service staff can move up."

Delegating Principles

Levels of delegation. Delegation is not an "all or nothing" situation. There are different levels of delegation, and a manager must determine to what degree they want to delegate authority. An effective manager understands that some tasks to be performed by others require only fact finding, while others may be followed through to completion. Here is a list of some of the various degrees of delegation:

- Investigate and report back. The subordinate gathers facts for the manager. The manager then takes appropriate action.
- Recommend action. The subordinate recommends action based on fact-finding or specialized knowledge. The manager evaluates the recommendation and takes appropriate action.
- Advise of action planned. The subordinate makes decisions based on investigation. The manager evaluates the decision and approves or disapproves the decision.
- Take action; advise of action taken. The manager gives subordinate control over decision taken. The manager requests to be kept informed as to the action taken.
- Investigate and take action. The manager allows the subordinate full control over decision and supports the decision.

When delegating, the manager should be aware of certain limitations or rules of delegation. First, the delegating manager must follow through and find out the results. This is important not only for the task itself but also for the manager's understanding of subordinates' capabilities.

Delegating managers also need to set standards of performance so that subordinates can track their progress toward completing the task. Managers must also develop ways by which to monitor subordinates' progress. Such monitoring may take the form of written reports or discussion in meetings.

The delegating manager relinquishes many operational tasks. Although this gives the manager more time for "managing," they are still responsible for the smooth running of the overall operation. By setting levels of operating performance, the manager can monitor the operation and be alerted to changes. "Spread the work around. Let people know exactly what you expect. Follow up. It works—but only if you are organized. I come in about one-half hour earlier than expected so that I can get a sense of what needs to be done," states Lisa Rinehart, manager of The American City Diner, located in Bethesda, Maryland.

To Do or to Delegate.

You now know the degrees of delegation as well as its advantages and limitations. Where do you go from here? Time log analysis should give managers a clear idea of how their time is being spent. Using the above guidelines, managers can then decide which tasks they must do and which can be delegated.

Marilyn Moats Kennedy[70] suggests that the manager segment tasks into three categories to help eliminate activities that clog one's day. In the first category is work that can only be prioritized and done by the manager. In the second is work that can be delegated immediately. In the third is work that someone else could (and should) be doing when there is someone capable of accomplishing the task. The manager should understand subordinates' capabilities so that work in the second category can be delegated and accomplished immediately. The nature and amount of work in the third category will identify the staff's training needs. As this training progresses, the manager will have more time for "managing." "I concentrate on utilizing my strengths. By recognizing what I am not good at doing, I can delegate to someone that has talent in those areas," states Jennifer Irwin, owner of Just A Taste restaurant in Ithaca, New York. Once these two categories of work have been addressed, the manager can concentrate on eliminating the "interrupters."

Eliminating Interruptions

Customer retention and business expansion are primary foci of most restaurant business plans. However, for many restaurants, actual work effort devoted to retention and expansion has fallen far short of goals. The primary reason for the lack of follow through on retention and expansion efforts stems from one of the ongoing dilemmas of time management: Critical activities often push aside the vital but non-critical activities of retention and expansion.[71] The day-to-day running of the restaurant gets in the way of primary goals and objectives. "In the day-to-day, you never know what is going to come up," states Mark Marotto, owner and manager of Marotto's restaurant in Kenmore, New York. "I plot, prioritize, and color code the daily, weekly, and monthly routine; but I have to schedule for the unexpected, too. At times, I have to 'just do it'—get rid of all the clutter to see the top of my desk."

The Phone Went Dead.

What can be done to eliminate frequent and unproductive interruptions in the workday? A well-trained assistant is the manager's first and most effective line of defense. The Ferguson/Berger study noted telephone calls as the most serious interrupter of all.[72] In fact, a recent survey found that the majority of small-company managers spend one to three hours a day on the telephone.[73] By screening calls, the assistant can prevent the majority of these interruptions for the manager. Since occasional emergencies and other situations do arise, the assistant should be able to distinguish important calls and be aware of key individuals the manager should speak with immediately. Another option is for assistants to take messages, thus allowing managers to fit return calls into their own schedules.

If managers becomes involved in unproductive phone conversations and the callers will not hang up, managers can experiment by using the "radical termination method" in which they hang up in the middle of one of their own sentences. Most callers will blame the disconnection on the phone company rather than assume that the manager was being rude. After all, who hangs up on themselves?

I Only Need a Moment.

The next most serious interrupter in the manager's workday is the unscheduled meeting or "walk-in" visitor. According to the Ferguson/Berger study, restaurant managers spend three and one-half times more of their day on unscheduled meetings than other managers (35 percent versus 10 percent).[74] Such meetings take up more of a restaurant manager's day than any other single activity. Consequently, they must be reduced to the point where the manager is once again in control of the workday. Again, the assistant can screen visitors and schedule meetings with the manager at a more convenient time. If the visitor insists on seeing the manager, the manager should come out of the office and meet the visitor on neutral ground, thus preventing the guest from sitting down and tying up a long period. Should the visitor persist in idle conversation—watch for nonverbal signs at the start such as such as leaning against a desk or a doorway and rocking back and forth—make the visitor aware of time limitations. As a next step, the manager can begin on-the-floor rounds, thus letting the visitor know cordially—but unmistakably—that time is finished. If that fails, a trip to the restroom will likely do the trick.

A Desk in the Rafters?

While an open-door policy is valuable for promoting open communications, the manager must have some uninterrupted work time. Many managers now find that it is beneficial to have a second office or a hidden retreat where they can work uninterrupted for extended periods. Although a second office is not common in the restaurant where space is usually at a premium, a desk or a table in the attic or the basement would work. If this is not possible, the manager should spend certain mornings working at home.

Meetings.

Scheduled meetings also proved to be a time user for the restaurant manager. The Ferguson/Berger study determined that restaurateurs conducted an average of 2.4 meetings lasting approximately 46.2 minutes long each per day.[75] This accounted for 29 percent of the entire day. We feel that meeting time could be reduced through planning and prioritizing the issues for meetings using the following strategies:

- Each time a meeting is held, a record of the time spent per person and the hourly salary of the persons attending should be kept. This can be tabulated to determine the total cost of the meeting and compared to the actual results or outcome of the meeting. If someone other than the manager calls the meeting, that person should be given a copy of the cost and analyze its impact of it on the daily operating performance. The astute manager will be able to determine if the benefits derived from the meeting outweigh the costs. The probable outcome will be fewer, more productive meetings.

- Be aware of meeting attendees with compound agendas. When a person has multiple issues, a list-making strategy can be employed. Taking brief notes forces the speaker to be clear and specific. Ending a rambling conversation positively, yet firmly, is a critical skill to develop.

- All too often, meetings are held on an open basis in order to receive as much input as possible. Sometimes this can cause them to become aimless and unstructured chat sessions instead of information forums. To reduce the chance of meetings from getting out of control, the manager and staff must be well prepared in advance. This task is in the control of the manager who can set up time limits and detailed agendas to follow, and assign persons to comment on certain topics.[76]

- Once the agenda is complete, the meeting should cease. If there are topics that have been addressed outside the agenda, the manager should schedule those topics on the next agenda. If the topic is of extreme importance, it should be discussed with the appropriate people after the meeting concludes. This way, people that will not be involved can return to their own tasks and not have their time wasted in a costly drain of resources. Before the meeting is adjourned, the manager should present a briefing as to the issues and responsibilities for the next meeting so each person will be prepared.[77]

Michael Furtado, regional manager of California Pizza Kitchen shared these ideas on meetings: "Monday staff meetings work well. We can communicate prior week results while events are still fresh on our minds. It also gives us an opportunity to make necessary adjustments for the upcoming week. Everyone is involved. I always keep a pad handy so I don't forget to note important issues."

Are Attendees Contributing?

The manager should also be aware of other peoples' time. How often have you been asked to attend a meeting that wasted your time? Often a copy of the minutes is as informative as the meeting itself. Keep this in mind whenever you schedule a meeting. Require attendance only of those who will be contributing to the agenda and ask others if they would like to attend. This will allow others to evaluate how the meeting will affect their time and will prevent anyone feeling overlooked.

If the meeting is informal, of short duration, and consists of only a few persons, the manager may elect to hold a stand-up meeting. When required to stand throughout the meeting, people tend to say only what really needs to be said. This will help ensure that the meeting does not go into "overtime."

Mounding Paperwork

Incoming paperwork is another problem faced by the restaurant manager. One day's absence from the desk can result in a stack of correspondence and memos that takes two days to sort and answer. People seem to take advantage of the manager's day off to overload them with unusual amounts of material. This perception is true in a sense because throughout a working day, the manager is constantly sending verbal replies to the queries of others.

The manager can eliminate a large portion of wasted time by reviewing all incoming paperwork. Shelly Branch focuses on Marriott International's CEO, Bill Marriott, who has a long-standing policy of handling "one piece of paper just once" before routing it or throwing it away.[78] Expanding on the Marriott method, Branch recommends that while managers review the paperwork, that they organize it into three categories: one that requires action, one that requires reading, and one that should be thrown out. When going through the first group (action category), the manager should respond to each one individually. Action should be taken before the next one is read. The second group (reading category) should be separated into two piles: those that require passing on and those that need filing. The third group should be discarded. The emphasis is on handling each piece of paper one time only. Nicole Melvin, restaurant manager of The Heritage House in Cincinnati, Ohio, shared her secret for keeping up to date with industry reading: "I scan the industry magazines for articles of interest and toss the rest. If I don't, they'll build up into a pile a mile high that I'll never get through."

Writing Reports

Sometimes reports submitted to the manager are of poor quality and too lengthy and need to be re-written. One study found that some department heads spend up to 40 percent of their time just in writing.[79] This writing process should be a tool for productivity, but is often a blockage: Writers waste time producing poorly written, laborious texts that waste even more time for managers. Here are some strategies that can help alleviate the restaurateur's burden of revising shoddy, long-winded reports:

- Have the person responsible redo the work.
- Set an atmosphere of excellence to help minimize problems in the future. Make it clear that you expect smart, simple, and short reports.
- Make sure the staff person understands the job requirements and timetables.
- Make sure people are not over-committed. Staff people have a tendency to say "yes" to every demand. Over-commitment leads to unfinished and sloppy work.
- Give or bring in an expert to give a one-day seminar on writing memos.

Spam

What about junk mail and e-mail? Once a manager is on one mailing list, amounts of spam seem to increase proportionally. An assistant can eliminate this problem also by opening all mail and forwarding all the important pieces. This can then be roughly sorted by the manager in order of importance and be dealt with appropriately. Another trick would be to use different forms of the restaurant or manager's name when subscribing to publications, ordering them through vendors, and other correspondence. This will identify the source of the incoming mail and will help the sorting process in terms of importance.

Limited Support

It's no secret that in most cases, only large, high-volume restaurants can afford an administrative support staff. Typically, restaurateurs operate in a self-contained mode. Here are some tactics managers can consider for dealing with interruptions when they do not have other staff members to whom they can delegate tasks:

- Use voice mail to screen calls. Return important calls in groups.
- Move the telephone or turn the ringer off so you cannot hear it ring.
- Use e-mail to help eliminate unnecessary calls

Summary

In this article, we have shown the manager how to break old habits, how to delegate tasks, and how to eliminate interrupters. With proper implementation, we are confident that even the worst time managers will benefit from these techniques. It all begins with the time log and a proper analysis of how time is spent. Though itself time-consuming, the time log will produce lasting benefits of better habits, more effective delegation, and fewer interruptions.

Where Managers go From Here

Managers must use the freed time to attend to more important tasks and projects including: planning, organizing, being creative, and leading. Managers must be prepared to take these new blocks of time and use them to plan for the future.

Hints for Effective Time Management

- Maintain a daily list of things to do; make a new one each day. Use a clipboard, a yellow pad, a daily planner— whatever works.

- Schedule quiet time for thinking, planning, and reflecting.
- Schedule slack time as a buffer.
- Group similar tasks.
- Vary your work schedule to include off-peak periods and work done away from the restaurant.
- Instill a climate of discipline in which everyone respects the keeping of time.
- Concentrate on your strengths.
- You cannot possibly read all of the industry magazines you receive; and you would probably be better off to stop trying.
- Keep a notepad handy.
- Avoid over-supervising. Let people make (and learn from) mistakes.
- Set short- and long-term goals including deadlines for each goal.
- Set priorities on a daily basis. Rank tasks in order of priority of importance.
- Work smart. Avoid excessive attention to low-yield tasks or projects; delegate to others.
- Avoid over-committing yourself. Do what you do well— like a craftsperson.
- Distinguish between the important and the urgent.
- 'Just do it'—avoid procrastination and perfectionism.
- Prioritize. Do first things first—including unpleasant, distasteful, or dreaded tasks.
- Encourage and empower team members to solve their own conflicts.
- Control interruptions (phone calls, meetings, drop-in visitors, etc.). Move from an open-door policy to a screen-door policy.
- Utilize, but do not waste time with computers. Wasting time includes activities such as re-configuring programs, on hold and on line time with technical support, and clearing out cluttered disk storage.

Delegation[80]

Questions:
Should I delegate to one person?
Should I delegate to a group?

When to delegate to an individual:
- They have pertinent information or appropriate skills.
- You need for them to comprehend and embrace the task.
- They can grow personally or professionally.
- Time is not a critical factor.
- The conflict risk is low.

When to delegate to a group:
- The interaction will add clarity to or help structure the problem.
- Interaction will help increase motivation.
- Conflict may lead to better solutions.
- Time is not a critical factor.
- Excessive conflict risk is low.

Questions:
Should I delegate decision-making authority to the group?
Should I participate with the group?

When to delegate:
- The group can perform competently and your time will be saved.
- The group's autonomy will increase their drive to perform well.
- The group has adequate information and talent to accomplish the task or project.

When to participate:
- No one else can provide the necessary leadership.
- The group needs information only possessed by you.
- Your presence will not disrupt the group process.
- Your time will be spent productively.

Endnotes

1 Gary K. Vallen, "Organizational Climate and Burnout," Cornell Hotel and Restaurant Administration Quarterly February 1993: 54.

2 Nelson, Debra L. and Quick, James C., Organizational Behavior (St. Paul, MN: West Publishing Company, 1994) 188.

3 Vallen "Organizational Climate and Burnout." 55.

4 H. J. Freudenberger, "Staff Burnout," Journal of Environmental Issues Number 30 1974: 159-65.

5 Christine Maslach, "Burned-out," Human Behavior Number 5 1976: 17-22.

6 Christine Maslach and Susan E. Jackson, Maslach Burnout Inventory Manual, 2nd edition (Palo Alto, California: Consulting Psychologists Press, 1986) 1.

7 Maslach and Jackson 1.

8 Maslach and Jackson 1.

9 Krone, Tabacchi, and Farber 58-63.

10 Maslach and Jackson 1.

11 Maslach and Jackson 2.

12 Maslach and Jackson 2.

13 Maslach and Jackson Maslach Burnout Inventory Manual.

14 Maslach and Jackson 2.

15 Maslach and Jackson 2.

16 Vallen "Organizational Climate and Burnout." 55.

17 Lang 138.

18 Lang 138.

19 The concept of bottom-up thinking as referred to by Lang suggests senior managers become slaves to managers; managers become slaves to employees; and employees become slaves to members.

20 Lang 138.

21 Gardner, M., The Annotated Alice: Alice's Adventures in Wonderland & Through the Looking Glass (New York: Clarkson N. Potter, Inc., 1960), p. 88.

22 Terpstra, David E. and Elizabeth J. Rozell. "The Relationship of Goal Setting to Organizational Profitability." Group and Organization Management. Vol. 19, No. 3, (September 1994), pp. 285-294.

23 Mesch, Debra J., Jiing-Lih Farh, and Philip M. Podsakoff. "Effects of Feedback Signs on Group Goal Setting, Strategies, and Performance." Group and Organization Management, Vol.19, No.3, (September 1994), pp. 309-333.

24 Locke, E. A. and Latham, G. P. A Theory of Goal Setting and Task Performance (Englewood Cliffs, NJ: Prentice Hall, 1990).

25 O'Hair, D. and Friedrich, G. W. (1992). Strategic Communication in Business and the Professions (Boston: Houghton Mifflin Company, 1992).

26 Stallworth, H. (1990, June). "Realistic goals help avoid burnout." HR Magazine, Vol. 35, 6, (June 1990), p. 171.

27 O'Hair 1992.

28 Shalley, Christina E. "Effects of Productivity Goals, Creativity Goals, and Personal Discretion on Individual Creativity." Journal of Applied Psychology, Vol. 76, No.2, (1991), pp. 179-185.

29 Latham, Gary P. and Edwin A. Locke. "Self-Regulation Through Goal Setting." Organizational Behavior and Human Decision Processes, 50, (1991), pp. 212-247.

30 Earley, Christopher P, William Prest, and Pauline Wojnaroski. "Task Planning and Energy Expended: Exploration of How Goals Influence Performance." Journal of Applied Psychology, Vol.72, No.1, (1987), pp. 107-114.

31 Locke, Edwin A. "The Determinants of Goal Commitment." Academy of Management Review, Vol.13, No.1, (1988), pp. 23-39.

32 Gatewood, R. D., Taylor, R. R., and Ferrell, O. C., Management Comprehension, Analysis, and Application. (Burr Ridge, IL: Richard D. Irwin, Inc., 1995).

33 Earley, 1987.

34 Earley, 1987.

35 Mathis, R. L. and Jackson, J. H. (1997). Human Resource Management. (St. Paul, MN: West Publishing Co., 1997).

36 Maier, Norman R. F. "Assets and Liabilities in Group Problem Solving: The Need for an Integrative Function." Psychological Review, Vol.74(4), (1967), pp.233-249.

37 Locke, 1988.

38 Zander, Alvin, The Purposes of Groups and Organizations. (San Francisco: Jossey-Bass, Publishers, 1985).

39 Gellatly, Ian R. and John P. Meyer. "The Effects of Goal Difficulty on Physiological Arousal, Cognition, and Task Performance." Journal of Applied Psychology, Vol.77, No.5, (1992), pp. 694-704.

40 Thompson, Jr., A. A. and Strickland III, A. J., Strategic Management Concepts and Cases. (Burr-Ridge, IL: Richard D. Irwin, Inc., 1995).

41 O'Hair, 1992.

42 Gilliland, Stephen W. and Ronald S. Lamis. "Quality and Quantity Goals in a Complex Decision Task: Strategies and Outcomes." Journal of Applied Psychology, Vol.77, No.5, (1992), pp. 672-681.

43 Locke, E. A., Chah, D., Harrison, S., and Lustgarten, N. "Separating the Effects of Goal Specificity From Goal Level." Organizational Behavior and Human Decision Making, 43, (1989), pp. 270-287.

44 Mitchell, Terence R. and William S. Silver. "Individual and Group Goals When Workers Are Interdependent: Effects on Task Strategies and Performance." Journal of Applied Psychology, Vol. 73, No. 2, (1990), pp. 185-193.

45 Mesch, 1994.

46 Mesch, 1994.

47 O'Hair, 1992.

48 Locke, 1989.

49 Locke, 1988.

50 Gellatly, 1992.

51 Locke, 1988.

52 Matthews, Linda M., Terence R. Mitchell, Jane George-Flavy, and Robert E. Wood. "Goal Selection in a Simulated Managerial Environment." Group and Organization Management, Vol.19, No.4, (December 1994), pp. 425-449.

53 Matthews, 1994.

54 Mesch, 1994.

55 Mitchell, 1990.

56 Locke, 1988.

57 Gordon, Jack, Hequet, Marc. and Stamps, David." We Realize You're Too Busy To Read This, But.... Training. Feb 1997, v34 n2, p. 20-22.

58 Macadam, Charles. "Do You Control Your Time—Or Does It Control You? Works Management. Jan 1997, v50 n1, p. 44-45.

59 Ferguson, Dennis and Florence Berger, "Restaurant Managers: What Do They Really Do?", Cornell Hotel and Restaurant Administration Quarterly, November 1984, pp. 26-36.

60 Merritt, Edward A. "Hospitality Management: A Study of Burnout." An unpublished Master of Business Administration research project, Pepperdine University, March, 1996, p. 15.

61 Liddle, Alan. "Look Beyond Foodservice For Learning Tools." Nation's Restaurant News. Jun 9, 1997, v31 n23, p. 74.

62 Ferguson and Berger, op. cit., p. 33.

63 Thrampoulidis, K. X., Goumopoulos, C. and Housos, E." Rule Handling in the day-to-day Resource Management Problem: An Object-Oriented Approach," Information & Software Technology, March 1997, pp. 185-193.

64 "The Multi-Department Management Maze." Food Management, Feb 1997, v32 n2, p. 24.

65 Mintzberg, Henry, Quinn, James Brian, and Voyer, John, The Strategy Process, Englewood Cliffs, NJ: Prentice Hall, 1995, p. 222.

66 "Caught In A Vicious Cycle?" Sales & Marketing Management. Jan 1997, v149 n1, p. 48-56.

67 Ferguson and Berger, op. cit., p. 31.

68 Spencer, Margaret S. "Overcoming Procrastination: How To Get Things Done Despite Yourself." Law Practice Management. Apr 1997, v23 n3, p. 51-53

69 Reynolds, Dennis. "Mitigating Managerial Burnout—Recognize the Symptoms and Take Remedial Action." Trumpet. Fall 1993, p. 12-13.

70 Kennedy, Marilyn Moats. "Rightsizing Your Job." Across the Board. Feb 1997, v34 n2, p. 53-54.

71 Phillips, Phillip D. "Business Retention And Expansion: Theory And An Example In Practice." Economic Development Review, Summer 1996, v14 n3, p. 19-24.

72 Ferguson and Berger, op. cit., p. 30.

73 Caggiano, Christopher. "All Talk No Action?" Inc. Jul 1997, v19 n10, p. 104.

74 Ferguson and Berger, op. cit., p. 31.

75 Ibid., p. 31.

76 "How To Save Time At Meetings." Management-Auckland. Nov 1996, v43 n10, p. 18.

77 Struebing, Laura. "Does Your Company Invest Your Time Wisely?" Quality Progress, Dec 1996, v29 n12, p. 10.

78 Branch, Shelly, " So Much Work, So Little Time.", Fortune, Feb 3, 1997, v135 n2, p. 115-117.

79 Neff, Richard E. "CEOs Want Information, Not Just Words So... Write Smart, Simple And Short. Communication World. Apr/May 1997, v14 n5, p. 22-25.

80 Adapted from Whetten, David A. and Cameron, Kim S. Developing Management Skills. New York City: HarperCollins Publishers, Inc., 1991, p. 116.

CPSIA information can be obtained at www.ICGtesting.com
Printed in the USA
LVOW07s0846300514

387924LV00002B/2/P